Volvo F88 & F89 at work

Second Edition

Patrick W Dyer

Old Pond
PUBLISHING LTD

ACKNOWLEDGEMENTS

There are many, many people without whose help this book would never have been published. Be it for the provision of photographs or those wonderful gems of information, which often linked a long chain of investigation, their contribution has been invaluable to the project. For their particular help, enthusiasm and support I would like to thank, in no particular order, the following: Del Roll, Peter Webb, Robert Clayden, Peter Riches, Nigel Hanwell, Jim Horn, Sue Chapman, John Comer, Adrian Cypher, Marcus Lester, George Bennett, Bob Rhead, Ulla Bergwall and of course my wife, Linda. If I have missed anyone out please accept my apologies.

ABOUT THE AUTHOR

Patrick Dyer, born in 1968, grew up during one of the most notable and exciting periods of development for heavy trucks and also the last of the real glory days for trucking as an industry. This is reflected in his subject matter. His previous books covered the LB110, 111 and 141 from Scania, the 2800, 3300 and 3600 from DAF and the Ford Transcontinental. This book is a revised second edition of Patrick's first book *Volvo F88 and F89 at Work*.

Although Patrick's day job is in motor sport, he holds a Class One licence and drives whenever the opportunity arises. He is also the proud owner of a 1983 Volvo F12, finished in the livery of Edwin Shirley Trucking, which he restored with the help of long-term friend, Ashley Pearce.

DECLARATION

There were at least six recognised methods of measuring engine output for trucks during the period covered by this book. Manufacturers and magazines often quoted different outputs for the same engine using BS.Au, SAE, DIN and ISO systems, some gross and some net, much to everyone's confusion. Therefore, for clarity, only the figures quoted by Volvo at the time are used throughout this work.

DEDICATION

I would like to dedicate this book to the memory of my father John Dyer. I wish you were here to read it.

Second Edition 2012

Copyright © Patrick W Dyer, 2005, 2012

1st edition pub. Gingerfold Publications, 2005

Patrick W Dyer has asserted his right under the Copyright, Designs and Patents Act, 1988, to be identified as the Author of this Work

ISBN 978-1-908397-15-7

A catalogue record for this book is available from the British Library

Published by
Old Pond Publishing Ltd
Dencora Business Centre,
36 White House Road
Ipswich IP1 5LT United Kingdom

www.oldpond.com

Front cover photograph
The F89 arrived in 1970 and immediately set the standard for modern super trucks. The new truck shared the F88's cab and was updated at the same time in 1973-4. Early examples, such as this, were identifiable by the single metal grab handle under the windscreen.
(Photo: AB Volvo Historical Archive)

Back cover photograph
This was one of the original running prototypes of the new F88 290 as tested on the open road by Volvo and is almost to production spec. The only significant difference is the mushroom cap fitted to the airstack, which is of a larger diameter than the final production item.
(Photo: AB Volvo Historical Archive)

Cover design and book layout by Liz Whatling
Printed and bound in China

Contents

Foreword

By George Bennett
Editor, Truck *magazine 1987-89 & 1990-97*

Volvo's legendary F88 was an icon of the trucking world in the 1970s and Patrick Dyer's book covers its history and development in admirable detail, accompanied by a fascinating collection of photographs, which alone are worth the price of admission. I found Patrick's description of the American connection particularly interesting. It's ironic that Volvo found the US market so impenetrable in the '60s and '70s, but was later able to assume a leading position in the country by the 'simple' expedient of buying a US company, and infiltrating Volvo values by the back door.

My first professional contact with the F88 was back in 1973, at AM Walker of Cosby, near Leicester, in my first truck driving job. Walker's were dyed-in-the-wool fans of the Gardner-Atkinson combination but were unable to get hold of any of the new straight-eight 240 hp Gardners because of a prolonged strike at the engine factory. Instead, Walker tried one of those new-fangled Volvo F88s, and that was the end of the Atki. It was a story repeated all across the British haulage industry. There was simply no contest – the gulf in technology represented by the arrival of Volvo (and Scania) was like the meeting of English settlers and Aboriginals in eighteenth-century Australia. We Atkinson drivers, on tip-and-load bonus, couldn't wait to get behind the wheel of an F88 that would cruise at 60-plus, haul up Loughborough bank at close to top speed, and supply us with a heater, a bunk and insulation from the engine in summer.

In the event I had to wait until 1978, at Cadwallader's in Oswestry, before I was given my first F88. It was a '290', which I drove for a week while its regular driver took a rare break. Having driven ERFs and Seddon Atkinsons with nine-speed Fuller gearboxes, the 16-speed Volvo was a revelation and, yes, the quiet and comfort were an extraordinary contrast. The gearshift and exhaust brake I had to work out for myself, since the only instruction I was given was: 'for God's sake watch the

brakes'. The weakness of the 290 in this area, particularly compared with the ERF I had been driving before, was made more apparent by the fact that the 290 could cruise at 75 mph, and frequently did. If Caddy drivers had no other tool, they at least had a 13 mm spanner to keep the trailer brakes adjusted up as far as possible, to compensate for the shortcomings up front.

The brakes, however, were the 290's only weakness; as a driver I couldn't have been happier, and I can recall that first F88 trip in considerable detail. I was hauling chocolate to the Mars factory at Hagenau in France, and I loved the gearshift (with its splitter set on the central console), the carpeted engine tunnel, the well-insulated cab walls and, above all, the speed and power of 290 hp at 32 tons. I went on to drive a variety of F88s at Cadwallader, including a three-day UK trip in NAW 500G, which we believed to be the first F88 in Britain. I didn't rate it much at the time, compared with my later-model 290, nor did I appreciate having the radiator header tank mounted in the cab and over the bunk, where it wept gently onto the toe of my sleeping bag. Years later, however, I saw the truck again at Volvo's UK headquarters in Warwick, where it had been splendidly restored. By now I was a tester at *Truck* magazine, and I tried hard to get a run in it, but the old 88 had become so valuable to Volvo that they wouldn't let anyone near it.

One of the great virtues of the F88 was its tight and predictable handling, particularly important when hauling hanging meat in a fridge trailer. I was reminded of this quite memorably in 1994, when I took part in a 'Trans Euro Test': a co-operation between six leading European trucking magazines that covered 1,400 km from Belgium to Italy. That year we tested four versions of Volvo's FH12, which had just been awarded the International Truck of the Year title. Alongside this test, we also compared an FH12 to a 10-year-old

F12 and a 20-year-old F89, the F88's more powerful brother. As the only member of the multinational test team who had worked with both of the older Volvo models as a regular driver, I was given the task of driving and reporting on all three generations of Volvo. It was one of the most enjoyable three days I spent in twenty years of truck testing.

Of course, the FH12 outshone the F12 and F89 in almost every respect – particularly in economy and comfort – and the F12 was noticeably better than the F89. But when it came to handling, the F89 had its more sophisticated descendants thoroughly beaten. The compact design of the cabin, and the lack of springing beneath it, made the F89 as tight through the bends as a go-kart. The realisation took me straight back to 1978 when, with a few colleagues at Cadwallader, I spent a summer belting to and from Italy, hauling peaches home. One day I was running with Dave Whitcombe, a driver not noted for hanging about, and who had just been given a new F10. I still had a trusty 290, only one frustrating registration number away from his new model, but when we came to the twisty old road into the Alps, between Mâcon and Chamonix, I had the unusual experience of leaving speedy Dave behind. I couldn't understand why, until we made a rare stop for coffee and he explained that his F10 just couldn't be hustled through the bends like an F88. It made be laugh then, and it made me smile fifteen years later when I recalled the incident during the Trans Euro Test.

It was a typical F88 moment, because the classic Volvo belonged to the days when truck driving was still fun, and crossing the Channel remained something of an adventure. For those of us brought up on the solid virtues of British trucks, among which driver appeal was notably lacking, the Volvo F88 was a truck to aspire to; along with the Scania 141, it was the truck everyone wanted to drive. I count myself lucky I was one of them.

GEORGE BENNETT

PREFACE to the SECOND EDITION

This revised edition of my first book was made possible by two important relationships, one with my publisher, the other with the manufacturer.

The first has seen my books produced in a polished and professional manner by the enthusiastic team at Old Pond. Their belief in my work is greatly appreciated.

The second relationship – with Volvo – started with an eleventh-hour request for help in providing key photographs for the first edition late in 2004. This has blossomed over the years, opening doors to the company's extensive archive and its knowledgeable staff. As a result, of the fifty-three new photographs in this edition Volvo provided thirty-three. This allowed the inclusion of examples from many countries other than the UK. In particular I was able to provide greater coverage of the G88 and G89 models which were rarely operated by UK-based firms and were infrequent visitors to these shores. Also featured are a rare prototype – which could have become the F88 290 – and a study of the cab interior that every driver aspired to work in.

Despite this new material, virtually all the original photographs have been retained – after all, if it ain't broke, don't fix it!

New documents and research material have allowed me to convey further information in new captions, revisions to old ones and additions to introductory chapters – some seven thousand extra words in all.

I hope that you enjoy reading this revised edition as much as I have enjoyed compiling it for you.

Patrick W Dyer 2012

Introduction

Project X, Where the Story Starts

To fully appreciate and understand the phenomenal success achieved by the Volvo System-8 family, and in particular the F88, it is important to go back to the early 1960s, a time of noisy and cramped cabs, crash gearboxes, heavy manual steering and harsh suspension. Truck design had moved on very little since the 1940s and the comfort, safety and well-being of the driver were very much of secondary importance after the dynamic abilities of the truck itself.

Volvo, who had been manufacturing trucks since 1927, was then producing a successful heavy truck range of a largely conventional design. These were commonly referred to at the time as 'Torpedos' due to the length and shape of their bonnets; the official designation of the heaviest was actually 'Titan'. These traditional, normal-control trucks had established an enviable reputation for their extreme ruggedness and durability while operating in the world's most inhospitable places from the frozen Arctic to searing desert. Unfortunately, the models on offer were largely unsuitable for the legislated transport systems that were starting to take shape throughout Europe. The recent introduction of the ISO container system had already made an impact on these countries and overall vehicle length now had to accommodate the maximum 40 ft (12 m) size of box which ruled out the use of most conventional tractor units.

Luckily for Volvo, development work on a solution for this particular problem was already well underway though, strictly speaking, it had been intended as the vanguard of an assault on the lucrative market in North America and not Europe.

Following the successful introduction of its car range into the USA in the mid 1950s, Volvo had tried in 1958-9 to establish its range of conventional trucks as well. The potential for export dollars from this vast market was a tempting carrot to any manufacturer and Volvo envisaged that success in the USA would fund their future development plans elsewhere. However, it soon became apparent that the American truck manufacturers, also struggling with strict overall length legislation dictated by ISO, were starting to favour the cab-over, or forward-control principle to overcome the new laws. These were typically equipped with a tilting mechanism for engine access. Although the tilt cab was yet to be adopted by European manufacturers, it was not a new idea in America. White were the first manufacturer commonly accredited with a mass-produced tilting cab, with the 3000 model of the late 1940s. It is somewhat ironic, given the importance of this innovation to both companies, that it was Volvo that acquired White's truck division in 1981.

To test the water, Volvo launched Project 2859 or X1 as it was known in-house. Several prototypes were assembled with some being shipped to America for field trials. These compact 4x2 tractors with extremely short BBC (Bumper to Back of Cab) dimensions featured a tilting cab, in both sleeper and short day-cab format, that already hinted at the eventual shape of the future F88. Volvo engineers dramatically improved on the basic tilting concept then available on American tractors and developed a cab that offered unrivalled comfort for the driver while still allowing engine access at least as good as that of contemporary conventional tractors. The design was also far simpler and cleaner than had previously been seen since all pipes, linkages and wiring runs were positioned as close as possible to the pivotal point at the front edge of the cab. Unfortunately, it became clear that the 2859 could not compete with the established domestic products, which enjoyed a fiercely loyal local market. The tare weight of the Swedish tractors was high when compared to the US products which made much use of aluminium and it would seem that the advantages of a frugal and efficient turbocharged engine were wasted on a country where fuel was both plentiful and cheap. With the project cancelled, the prototypes were returned to Sweden. However, armed with fresh ideas, and having learned some valuable lessons, Volvo engineers set out to design a new super truck, this time aimed squarely at Europe and the rest of the world.

One of the 2859 prototypes in day-cab format and looking very American in its configuration with its very short BBC dimensions, Trilex spoked wheels, cylindrical tank, West Coast mirrors and utilitarian front bumper. However, the F88 ancestry is clearly evident especially when compared to the G88 derivative which featured a set forward front axle position. Note that the familiar Volvo grille slash, first seen in the 1920s, made a temporary reappearance on these prototypes but was not to be seen on a production model until the F10/12 range of 1977.

(Photo: AB Volvo Historical Archive)

Volvo L4951 Titan TIPTOP
Laying the Foundations

A special project group developed the L4951 Titan TIPTOP outside the usual truck range. The group was instructed to use only the best components then available from the existing Titan, to produce a true flagship model with a cab-over design. The engine was to be the established TD96, a powerful and efficient turbocharged unit of 9.6 litres displacement, that developed (for the time) a staggering 230 bhp. This engine had roots that stretched back to 1951 but it had been designed and strengthened from the outset to handle forced induction within its lifetime. Volvo had been among the first manufacturers to experiment with turbocharging and had envisaged it as the way forward once compressor technology had reached the point at which it could reliably be installed on a vehicle. By 1955 Eberspatcher of Germany, among others, had solved the problems of variable operating speed that had previously caused problems for exhaust-driven turbocharged engines. It was their unit that was chosen to transform the 150 bhp D96 into the 185 bhp TD96 (T denoting Turbo) with only a minor weight penalty of 25 kg. By 1964, compressor technology had advanced further still and the TD96 could now deliver the 230 bhp that the engineers required for the L4951.

The cab for the new vehicle, initially only available as a sleeper, was clearly a development of that used on the 2859 prototypes and was by now clearly recognisable as that of the forthcoming F88. For Europe this was to be a milestone in heavy truck design and its impact would be far reaching. Because servicing could be done with the cab tilted there was no longer any need for engine access panels in the cab floor. This allowed the crew to be more effectively sealed off from the goings-on beneath them, which meant that interior noise levels were drastically reduced and, accordingly, so too was driver fatigue. There were also sprung seats, adjustable to weight, which worked with rubber cab mounts to isolate as much vibration as was possible – basic now when compared to modern cab suspension systems – but in 1964 most cabs were still rigidly mounted to the chassis.

The strict Swedish safety laws meant that the cabs were immensely strong too. The all-steel construction was a far cry from the wooden-framed techniques still used by some manufacturers. The sense of security that this gave drivers was an enormous benefit to Volvo and did much to nurture the extraordinary driver appeal that the marque enjoys to this day. Another plus for the occupants was a powerful twin-heater system which was designed to cope with Sweden's northerly latitude and cold winter climate. This feature was something of a revelation to drivers at a time when heat soak from the engine was the best they could hope for in terms of winter warmth, and that was usually only available after the radiator had been blocked off with cardboard!

Operators were quick to appreciate the benefits too. The vast improvements in service down time that the tilting cabs provided meant a useful improvement in profitability.

As all these innovations arrived wrapped up in one package, it is little wonder that the L4951 Titan TIPTOP was so well received by such a technology starved industry. Volvo, the producers of those tough Third World capable products, was suddenly raised to an exalted position in the very top echelon of Europe's heavy truck manufacturers. In a brief twelve-month production life, around 1,500 examples of the L4951 were produced in both 4x2 (L4951) and 6x2 (L4952) formats.

However, Volvo, never a company to rest on its laurels, was already looking to the future and about to launch an ambitious plan. Titled System 8, this plan was to cover the redevelopment of the eight key components of engine, gearbox, axles, frame, steering, brakes, suspension and cab across the entire Volvo range to create the finest trucks then on offer.

The cornerstone of this redevelopment was to be the legendary F88, which went on to conquer all world markets to which it was made available.

Visually, the cab of the L4951 Titan TIPTOP differed from the subsequent F88 only in minor details such as the indicator design and location, cab marker lights and the absence of any badging apart from the Volvo grille emblem. The small fuel tank was the standard item and was the same for tractors. Note the small grille vent behind the door which fed air to the heater. This feature was carried over to the first F88s but was soon deleted. (Photo: AB Volvo Historical Archive)

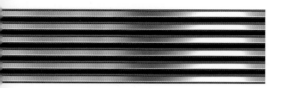

Volvo F88
World Beater

As it first appeared in 1965, the F88 was a much reworked and refined version of the L4951. Crucially the 230 bhp TD96 had been replaced by the all-new TD100 which provided a useful output of around 240 bhp. There was also the option of the normally aspirated D100 which gave around 100 bhp less – needless to say this was not a popular choice. Although it retained the 9.6-litre displacement of the TD96, the TD100 was nonetheless a brand-new engine, featuring a specially reinforced block to sustain higher outputs than before and individual cylinder heads for each of the six pistons. This approach was taken since the TD96, with ever-increasing output over the years, had become susceptible to the failure of head gaskets. For the TD100 the turbo compressor was provided by Schwitzer-Holset, a high-quality unit with a maximum running speed of 70,000 rpm, which was lubricated by force-fed oil from the engine.

A new gearbox, designated R60, was to provide eight fully synchromeshed gears. These were laid out in a simple-to-use double-H pattern and, to make life even simpler, gears 5-8 were generally the only ones required over 15 mph or so. The R60 was a range-change type unit and the selection from high to low was operated by a rocker switch mounted on the gearstick. Provision was made on the gearbox housing for two power take-off points (later three), one on the side of the casing and one on the rear, both of which were operated by compressed air and were controlled from the driver's seat.

The final drive systems followed Volvo's established philosophy of double reduction to extend component life and improve efficiency. As before, two options were offered. First, and most popular for fast highway use, was the double reduction rear axle assembly originally designated 181. This tough, compact unit utilised a 13-inch crown wheel in front of the differential gears for the first stage of reduction and was capable of operation at around 48 tons. It was also a very compact unit which offered good ground

clearance. For heavier work up to 70 tons, Volvo offered the 1841 axle with hub reduction. This used a 16.5-inch crown wheel for the first stage of reduction combined with bevel gears in the hubs for the second. In both cases the crown wheels utilised helical teeth (hypoid) to maximise the contact area and increase the lifetime of the unit. A selection of final drive ratios were available to match varying operational requirements.

There was also an air operated differential lock, which was engaged via a toggle switch on the dashboard. Three drive layouts were available: 4x2, 6x2 and 6x4. A six-wheeled chassis was designated FB88 (B standing for bogie) in sales material and specifications, but the vehicles were not badged as such. However, the early double-drive variants did wear a distinct '6x4' badge on the grille.

All these major components were contained within a new and improved chassis frame. Heavier side members with larger webs gave superior strength and better flexibility while the chassis top was smooth and of uniform height to ease the mounting of bodywork. Long-wheelbase rigids were also equipped with a 45-ton capacity towing member at the rear for drawbar operation.

More innovations appeared on the suspension with the introduction of progressive springing. At the front, semi-elliptical leaf springs became stiffer under load as the rear contact point could move on a slipper arrangement, thus shortening the spring length and increasing its resistance. There was also assistance from double-acting hydraulic shock absorbers. At the rear, on the 4x2 models, the main spring was backed up by a helper spring mounted above, which would only come into play as load increased. On the helper spring, both front and rear contact points could move as more load was applied.

With a notable increase in performance, it was decided that the braking system should be further enhanced with a third independent circuit. All three circuits ran from a Westinghouse compressor with four chassis-mounted reservoir tanks. Combined with an efficient exhaust brake and separate trailer circuit, this system gave the F88 trend-setting stopping ability.

Steering was via a ZF power-assisted recirculating ball system with an impressive 3.6 turns from lock to lock. Allied to the generous 40-degree front wheel arc, this gave the F88 superb manoeuvrability. A typical 4x2-tractor unit with a 3,200 mm wheelbase had an impressive turning circle of just 12 m, or 39 feet, which was achievable with low driver input.

To top off this remarkable package, Volvo transplanted (virtually unaltered) the cab of the L4951 Titan TIPTOP. Volvo was now producing the all-steel unit at the old Nystrum plant in Umea on the north-east coast of Sweden. Nystrum had been development partner and supplier for the original L4951 cab and, indeed, that of the Viking TIPTOP (F86), but Volvo had by now acquired the business for themselves. The Umea plant also manufactured the diesel and air tanks along with various other pieces of chassis hardware. Volvo was now manufacturing even more components than before. Engines, gearboxes, frames, brake drums, drive shafts and cabs were all under their control. This unique position gave an enviable edge over rivals for quality control and supply. Design changes and improvements were also far easier to implement, so development work could be on-going without any major disruption to production.

The F88 changed very little over its production life, a clear testament as to the quality of Volvo's original design and how far ahead of the competition it was in the first place. Perhaps the most notable development was that of the G88 which appeared in 1970. This model featured a set-forward front axle which increased the legal payload in some countries, notably Sweden

and Australia. When combined with the short day cab, which also appeared that year, the G88 made an ideal platform for high-cube loads and many were operated as wagon and drag outfits for just that reason.

Between 1965 and 1977 Volvo produced a staggering 40,000 examples of all types. Each one of these played a significant part in building an enviable reputation for reliability, performance, quality and safety which Volvo still enjoys to this day.

Bearing the 1968 registration, OAD 109F, this smart unit belonging to WG Golding and Sons must have been one of the very first F88s imported into the UK. It was based in Wootton-under-Edge but is seen here in 1971 running empty on the A4. Identifying features of these early examples were the top-mounted wipers, small mirrors and chrome grille with plain service panel below; the latter would prominently carry the VOLVO legend before long.

(Photo: Adrian Cypher)

Making a wonderful TIR pair, these F88s were typical of the era which witnessed the explosion of overland routes throughout Europe and beyond. To succeed on these extended routes a truck had to be powerful, comfortable and, above all, reliable. Although the two units are Dutch registered, the trailers are British owned and rented. However, the matching livery suggests more than a casual hire. Note the larger, non-standard diesel tanks fitted to this pair.

(Photo: AB Volvo Historical Archive)

W Carter, the container specialist, ran up to thirty F88s. VRT 505G was one of the earliest, a 1969 example with the 8-speed R60 gearbox that was operated under the fleet name 'Deben Wayfarer'. The naming of Carter vehicles dates back to 1965 when an AEC Mandator became 'Deben Viking'. The tradition continues to this day and still uses the Deben prefix as the company headquarters is on this river. Another feature of early F88s is the prominent grab handle mounted on the bulkhead in front of the passenger seat. (Photo: Adrian Cypher)

Although subsequently converted into a wrecker, this F88 240 started out as a 4x2 unit in 1968-9. Powerful tractor units of the day will always be converted to perform this essential role. SKR 289G is equipped with the basic style of lifting gear and bodywork that was often fitted by haulage companies to perform the recovery of their own vehicles. The base tractor in these cases would often be an ex-fleet vehicle that had been withdrawn from daily service. Interestingly, the rear of the cab has been fully glazed in this case, presumably a modification to assist rearward vision in its new role. Now rescuing coaches, SKR 289G is pictured at the Dorset Steam Fair in 2001.

(Photo: Len Jefferies)

JBH 392K was one of a number of F88s based at the Thame depot of FC Bennett and was a typical example of this well-presented fleet in the 1970s. Note that this unit, registered on a K-plate, is fitted with the larger mirrors that became standard that year and also the new air intake arrangement behind the cab. The latter had been developed for the F89 which appeared in 1970, but was also applied to the F88. Originally the turbocharger had drawn air through a filter housing mounted on the chassis beside the engine, but from chassis number 2764 this changed to the F89 snorkel type system and that roughly coincided with the later of the J-registered F88s. This clutch of Bennett vehicles is pictured at the 'Lorry Driver of the Year' contest in 1974 in which JBH 392K took part. *(Photo: Adrian Cypher)*

Barry Ives Haulage ran this and two other F88 240s. All three were early examples disposed of by FC Bennett from their Oxford depot. The units were just three years old but had been worked hard, regularly clocking 3,000 trunk miles a week. The workload for Barry was no easier as the units were kept busy on general haulage duties throughout the UK for a further six years before replacement. Pictured in 1981, GBH 445K waits to tip its interesting machinery load.

(Photo: Barry Ives)

Parked up with a full load of timber in 1977 and looking in fine fettle for a hard worked vehicle of around five years of age is this F88 240 of Woodcock's. Although F88s were generally referred to by their engine output (240 or 290) this model's actual designation would have been F88-32, the 32 relating to the wheelbase of 3,200 mm which was the most common length for UK 4x2 units. There were a further six wheelbase options available up to 4,600 mm.

(Photo: Adrian Cypher)

GHT 268K was operated out of Avonmouth by Harding Bros. Pictured in 1973 this heavily decorated F88 240 was the charge of George Briley who drove it all over the Continent with loads of ships' provisions. Note that the cab is fitted with the optional double bunk, as is evidenced by the largely obscured back window. The double bunk option allowed a single driver to leave one made up as a bed, while the other provided easy-to-hand storage. The only down side of the double-bunk arrangement was the drastically reduced headroom in what was already a very snug birth. *(Photo: Adrian Cypher)*

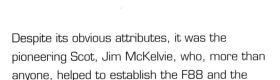

Jim McKelvie
A Helping Hand

Despite its obvious attributes, it was the pioneering Scot, Jim McKelvie, who, more than anyone, helped to establish the F88 and the Volvo brand in the UK.

McKelvie was a shrewd businessman, noted for his sense of humour, with many friends throughout the haulage industry. Following de-nationalisation, he had developed the family transport business into a major concern before selling it to the Transport Development Group (TDG), who continued to operate it under the well-known 'McKelvie' name and livery.

By 1967 McKelvie was looking for a new venture and, having noted the mediocre products available from British manufacturers, he decided that importing modern vehicles from one of Europe's up-and-coming producers would be the best way forward. It is believed that his initial inquiries were directed at MAN, but happily it was a deal made with Volvo to import the F86 that was to determine the future.

McKelvie, as an ex-haulier, knew that the Volvo product was very good. But more than that, he understood what was needed: a slick, efficient service network to support the new vehicles. This thinking was in sharp contrast to the complacent attitude of the domestic manufacturers to whom

'aftercare' was a low priority. McKelvie's new company, Ailsa Trucks, was to provide just that support from its Barrhead base. Drivers were given an emergency telephone number that put them in touch with a twenty strong, countrywide network of service outlets. This, and 24-hour parts availability, provided Volvo's new customers with complete peace of mind and was a fundamental part of the company's growth in the UK.

The first vehicle imported in 1967 was LNL 465E, the 4x2 F86 tractor famously belonging to T Hutchinson. A further 164 units followed that year. In 1968, the first F88s started to appear too and by 1972 the import total had reached 2,000 vehicles. Ailsa Trucks also started to assemble selected chassis the same year. In 1974, Jim McKelvie sold his remaining shares to Volvo and moved on to a new project, the Stonefield off-road vehicle. His legacy, after just seven years, was the number-one market position in the heavy sector and Volvo's largest export market.

When Jim McKelvie died in 1977 the industry lost a highly regarded and visionary figure. With the changing times, his like was not to be seen again.

This delightful early F88 240 of W Carman and Sons was part of their extensive continental fleet which operated under the Brit European title. Note the catwalk diesel tank and the different arrangement of the chassis hardware as this unit is fitted with a spare wheel carrier (although no spare wheel) between the batteries and air tanks. There also seems to be some problem with the passenger side wiper! (Photo: Adrian Cypher)

JTD 106K was part of the Robert Armstrong fleet in the 1970s. This Liverpool-based firm specialised in the bulk delivery of beer, wine and spirits throughout Europe using tanker trailers. Despite being fitted with the new larger mirrors, the driver of this F88 240 has augmented his rearward vision with an additional after-market item. The Armstrong fleet was later to be absorbed by the mighty Peninsular and Oriental Steam Navigation Company, or P&O to you and me. The company was still self-governing and the units, although running in the P&O blue and white, retained the Robert Armstrong name. (Photo: Adrian Cypher)

As well as extensive activity throughout Europe, the Carman fleet was also prolific on the Middle East run for which high-cube F88 drawbar combinations such as this were typically used. Interestingly, the van trailer on this combo is running on a separate dolly that has just been backed underneath, hence the lowered landing legs, so could also be towed by an articulated unit. Pictured in 1975, OMB 195L, washed and fuelled, is preparing to depart for the Middle East from the company's Trowbridge depot.
(Photo: Adrian Cypher)

Dennis Oates and Sons has always maintained a small but beautifully formed fleet from its Penzance base. Of the ten to twelve units on the books in the 1970s and '80s, five were F88s. Seen here at the company's Long Rock depot in 1980 is HAF 664L, an F88 240 with the 16-speed gearbox. This unit worked well into the 1980s and remains with the company. Being post-1973, it benefits from the fitment of electric windscreen wipers mounted at the bottom of the screen rather than the previous vacuum type fitted at the top which were prone to running out of puff at the most inopportune moment. *(Photo: Marcus Lester)*

In contrast is PMA 866L, a similar truck, but equipped with a regular drawbar trailer, which has just returned from a Middle East trip still wearing a film of baked-on desert dust. Note the extra 66-gallon diesel tank fitted to 'up' the vehicle's range and the Hatcher sun visor across the top of the windscreen to provide some relief to the driver. Just visible behind is a more humble Seddon used for domestic work. *(Photo: Adrian Cypher)*

Netherlay-based haulier, Tom Shanks, started out in 1972 with one F86 tractor unit and a flatbed trailer. However, specialising in the movement of equipment for Aberdeen's lucrative oil market allowed quick and sustained growth and the first F88 soon arrived. The star of the TST fleet was this pristine 1972 F88 240, a pre-update model with chrome grille and vacuum wipers. This extraordinary unit had spent its first 16 years in storage as part of a private collection of tractors, trucks and cars housed in an aircraft hangar in East Anglia. Being a complete time capsule, it was restricted to local work and truck-show outings. In the latter role it excelled, winning many prizes including 'Best Volvo Truck in the Country' on one occasion. When it was sold in the late 1990s, TAM 489 (the number plate in this picture is incorrect) had covered a mere 19,000 miles in 25 years! *(Photo: Tom Shanks)*

The fruit and vegetable distributors M and P Thody were based in Graveley, Cambridgeshire and can claim a true first with their F88 240, GNV 875L. This 4x2 unit was purchased new from the John Billows Volvo dealership and was the first articulated truck operated by an independent grower/distributor to be taken into London's Spitalfields Market – a remarkable statement at the time. The 1973 outfit was a regular sight on the roads between London and Cambridgeshire making the journey twice a week until it was retired in the mid 1980s. *(Photo: Mark Thody)*

Being laid up in the corner of a yard is usually the beginning of the end for old trucks. However, GNV 875L was lucky and found a saviour in Simon Carpenter. Simon, together with his brother Michael, had been searching for an original F88 with the 240-bhp engine as a restoration project. The pair were delighted when they answered a small ad and found Thody's completely original and under-worked unit. A deal was struck and GNV 875L found a new home with the rest of the Carpenters' fleet in Wiltshire. It also found a temporary new career as circumstances landed it with the unglamorous role of yard shunter. However, within a year it was laid up again to preserve it for restoration and the search for parts was on with Carpenter's drivers briefed to scour the country for suitable donors. The project moved slowly until Simon, recovering from a bad accident, could devote more time to it. The detailed restoration that followed resulted in this stunning unit. Finished in Carpenter's smart, traditional green-and-cream livery, GNV 875L has, after a brief return to work, become a firm favourite at truck shows. *(Photo: Len Jefferies)*

Westbound on the M4 in 1982 with an impressive load of straw is PHV 21L, an FB88 240 with 6x2 drive. Note the load supports running up from the bumper which were removable to allow cab tilting. An F88 chassis like this, with a 24-ton GVW (gross vehicle weight), would tip the scales at around 8.5 tons, depending on spec. Under the legislation of the time, this drawbar combination could have provided a competitive payload of around 21 tons.
(Photo: Marcus Lester)

'Home to roost.' This wonderful Saturday morning shot of the Syms yard catches a small portion of the fleet at rest including the company's two early F88 240s, PMR 720H and, slightly obscured in the background, NMW 619G. Even the earliest F88s, which were more basic than subsequent examples, must have seemed light years ahead of the contemporary, domestic machines that Syms were operating at the time. (Photo: Adrian Cypher)

Hopefully not a hanging load for this early F88 240 of Taunton Meat Haulage as it negotiates a roundabout with some vigour! Despite favouring the products of Mercedes-Benz, Magirus-Deutz and Fiat, Taunton Meat Haulage also ran the odd F86 and a few F88s, one of which later ended up with RT Keedwell. This large and respected fridge fleet was later to become Langdon Industries. *(Photo: Adrian Cypher)*

Barbour European evolved from Barbour Haulage whose first vehicle took to the road in 1924. The company grew steadily and with the explosion of continental traffic in the 1960s became a familiar sight on Europe's many new TIR trade routes. The F88 was a natural choice in this role and the Stirling-based fleet soon swelled with examples of the new machines from Sweden. Wearing Barbour's livery with a distinctive up and over scheme of white, orange and blue stripes, the F88 units were always well turned out. In this glorious picture, eight of the fleet line up, between cloudbursts, below Stirling Castle. This superb study highlights the detail modifications of new grille, wiper location, grab handles and badging which Volvo gradually introduced to the F88 range in a series of updates through 1973-4.

(Photo: Whyler Photos/Barbour European)

PWX 554M, 'The Chelworth Queen', may have started its career with Smith & Robinsons of Leeds. However, by 1980 it was one of a handful of vehicles operated by AJ Giles who specialised in moving anything that fitted into a bulker, particularly scrap metal. There is a little visual confusion with this unit as the correct black plastic grille has been painted silver to give a retro effect! *(Photo: Adrian Cypher)*

Pictured 'on the way out' and complete with lovely period 2-axle tilt is another view of Barbour's smart post-update unit, OWG 395M. Equipped with the TD100 engine producing 240 bhp and the 16-speed SR61 gearbox, this was exactly the long-distance, express haulage role that suited the F88 so well and which endeared it to so many operators.

(Photo: Whyler photos/Barbour European)

Big tractor units from the best of the European manufacturers and fitted with the biggest engine option available were the order of the day for the smart fleet of DJ Light, so it was no surprise to find examples of Volvo's finest in the company's smart green-and-cream livery. PYA 658L, a tidy F88 240, is pictured waiting in the yard with an impressive load of ARC concrete pipes stacked on its flatbed trailer. The year is 1975. *(Photo: Adrian Cypher)*

Despite the Q-plate we can safely identify this pristine wrecker as a very early example by its wipers, grille and lack of an air stack. Still a working vehicle when photographed in 1996 at Rivington services on the M61, it is remarkably well preserved. Note the deep-section, chrome-finished bumper of American origin and the replacement mirrors. *(Photo: Marcus Lester)*

Heanor Haulage used this interesting FB88 6x2 rigid for machinery removals. NPP 395M was purchased second hand and ready converted with a 'Fassi' hydraulic arm. The very specialised fleet included around seven F88s at this time as well as a rare, for the UK, G88 6x2 unit. Heanor, with the exceptional nature of its work, found it advantageous to replace the SR61 gearboxes of both its F88 and F89s with Fuller 9 or 13-speed constant mesh items. These conversions were carried out by the company's own extremely competent workshop. *(Photo: Adrian Cypher)*

Tony Millard dreamed of owning an F88 when they were introduced. Twenty years later, in 1988, he was able to realise his dream. However, JVY 362L was not destined to join his successful tipper fleet that worked the quarries around Bristol but, instead, it would provide the traction for his fast-growing CB business 'Rig N Twigs'. The unit was a part-customised F88 240 that had already undergone a chassis stretch and gained a lift axle. The stretch allowed Tony to accommodate the truck's star feature, a massive aerodyne style sleeper box complete with sink, shower and television. Finished in sumptuous deep-buttoned blue velour, the box provided cosy accommodation for Tony and his crew while at shows. The rest of the unit received equal attention with the cab having a luxury interior in the same velour trim. Outside were twin custom exhaust stacks, cylindrical diesel tanks, a custom bumper and numerous one-off pieces of trim beautifully crafted in stainless steel. Pictured on its first outing, the truck actually developed further gaining encased stainless steel steps that blended into the bumper, a stainless housing at the back of the chassis to accommodate the rear lights, number plate and VOLVO legend and wheel trims. *(Photo: Len Jefferies)*

As Radclive Transport had horticultural roots (no pun intended), the company's logo incorporated this distinctive leaf emblem. This fine line-up features just a few of the many F88s that the company operated on general haulage to destinations throughout the UK, Europe and Middle East. Despite all four of these well-travelled units being L-registered, they illustrate well the changes that occurred through 1973-4. In addition to the new grille, wipers and grab handles at the base of the windscreen, the second unit in also has the latest style of bumper with two foot-holds cut out.

(Photo: Adrian Cypher)

Fresh from the paint shop, BHR 299L of Swindon Transport finds itself employed on bulker work before the sign writing could be applied in 1973. This was just one of the smart F88 240s that was operated by the McLindsay brothers from the company base in Lydiard Millicent. The F88 had a design capability of 48 tons, a useful margin over the F86 which only just made the UK's 32-ton limit, and so offered operators a great performance advantage over the smaller machine.

(Photo: Adrian Cypher)

In 1970 Volvo introduced the G88 derivative that featured a new front axle location 30 cm ahead of the standard F88. The G88 was developed to allow legal operation in countries requiring wider axle spacing but was made available to all markets. Of all the System 8 products it was the G88, particularly when fitted with a day cab, which most closely resembled the 2859 prototypes of the early 1960s. Hays bought fifty 4x2 G88s as the layout allowed a gross 32-ton load while remaining legal. This example was one of many that hauled these small-diameter tankers, for china clay, up and down the M5.

(Photo: Adrian Cypher)

Quinnen and Coles operated this well-worked FB88 on round-timber haulage. The unit was equipped with a hefty hydraulic arm for self-loading and is pictured westbound on the M4 in 1983. Visible in this picture is the roof hatch that first appeared in 1971. Drivers were provided with a welcome source of ventilation by the addition of this three-position item. It was the very short BBC (bumper to back of cab) dimension of the F88 day cab which allowed this example to be mounted with such a substantial self-loading device without affecting the coupling clearance of the trailer and load.

(Photo: Marcus Lester)

Don't judge a book by its cover for when the author caught up with the last of Hays' G88s in the summer of 1997, the thirty-year-old unit was still working around the clock shunting trailers. One drawback of the G88's axle position was the harsh ride characteristics suffered by drivers as a result of the shortened springs. However, during a fleeting break for the camera, this vehicle's driver, Tracy, informed the author that she loved the old G88 and far preferred it to the modern Tugmasters on the site. Just visible on the back of the front mudguard are the relocated cab steps. *(Photo: Author)*

As kingpin position and trailer clearance do not appear to be an issue with this particular combination, it is reasonable to assume that the weight of load dictated the use of a G88 chassis for this application. Of course, the sturdy nature of the trailer, with its quadruple four-in-line axle arrangement, and the overall colour scheme point to military use and most likely tank transport. The unit can be identified as a 1973 example as it has the re-positioned wipers introduced that year but not the black grille of 1974. By 1971 the Swedish army had taken delivery of 300 of its new MBT (main battle tank), the unique Stridsvagn 103B, or S-tank as it was generally known. Volvo provided key elements of the tank's drivetrain, so maybe the transporter evolved through that connection. *(Photo: AB Volvo Historical Archive)*

Remember the days before small, neat satellite dishes when the only way to get a fuzzy picture on your black and white portable television was with an aerial like this? Probably among the last of the chrome-grilled F88s to be registered, this well cared for example was at least ten years old when photographed dropping into Dover. Modifications include a catwalk diesel tank, large roof spoiler and the fitting of an F88 290 cylindrical air stack. *(Photo: David Wakefield)*

This 4x2 unit was an imported European-spec F88 operated by RD Trucking. As such, it was the usual combination of TD100 engine, SR61 gearbox and double-reduction back axle, but the lights with yellow lenses, width markers and roof rack gave the unit a distinctly European look. Pictured in 1981, EHY 26W looks well travelled. Note the modified air intake, which looks rather home made. *(Photo: Marcus Lester)*

Could Volvo's engineers have ever envisaged such longevity from the original design? Still working after nearly forty years, and on tough round-timber haulage at that, this late chrome grille example stands testament to the F88's straightforward and reliable mechanical components. The F88's distinct split screen was cheaper and easier to produce than a one-piece item and brought operators cost reductions when replacement was required if only one side was affected. The joining strip in the middle was so subtle it posed no hindrance to forward vision. *(Photo: Clive Davis)*

Australia presents some unique problems to truck manufacturers with its sheer size, wildly varying climate and tough outback conditions. Volvo, along with other European manufacturers, started to make inroads to this market in the 1960s by vying for business with popular trucks from the USA and Great Britain. Legislation operated along the lines of the American system where 'bridged weight' was all-important and enforced via a network of weighbridges. As such, interesting axle layouts, like the trailer on this example, were widely adopted. Although this is a standard F88, Volvo did well in this market with the G variant for just this reason. *(Photo: AB Volvo Historical Archive)*

A key part of the F88s success was the superb cab, which was essentially that of the L4951 Titan TIPTOP first introduced in 1964. This innovative design made the transition to the F88 chassis virtually unchanged, and was the first in Europe to offer a tilting facility. It was also very strong as a result of Sweden's tough impact laws. With no need for engine access panels inside, it also offered drivers an unusually quiet work place.

A high level of comfort was provided inside by a powerful twin-heater system that was developed by the Volvo engineers to combat the extreme conditions found in Sweden. The main unit was mounted on the bulkhead in front of the passenger seat and heated that side of the cab as well as handling windscreen and side window de-misting. This unit, positioned directly behind the flap vent in the front of the cab – so often seen in the open position – drew fresh air in from outside. The second heater unit was installed directly below the driver's seat, and blew hot air out onto his or her feet – great if you had wet and cold footwear. However, this unit drew air from within the cab and the flap on the driver's side of the cab was just a fresh air vent; it is rare to see both open together as is illustrated here. Drivers greatly appreciated this sophisticated heating system and found that the cab would be warm within a mile of the yard, even in the most severe conditions. Sporting a smart Scottish livery, this handsome F88 240 of W & D Gammie is pictured tipping a load of finest Aberdeen beef at London's Smithfield Market in 1976.

(Photo: Truck magazine)

When first faced with the problem of moving large prefabricated concrete loads, innovative Somerset haulier Ray Gillard opted to fabricate bogies in-house from the chassis of old tipper trucks. Eight-leggers were favoured for the twin-steering arrangement and provided a very strong and highly manoeuvrable bogie for the self-supporting loads. This smart FB88 240 is a 6x2 unit with the SR61 gearbox, double-reduction differential and air-lift rear axle. A number of identical units joined the Gillard's fleet in the mid 1970s replacing 6x4 machines from other manufacturers that were too heavy when on general haulage. As well as the useful weight saving, the legendary reliability of the TD100 engine was a key purchasing factor as contracts to move bridge beams, for instance, carried huge penalties for late delivery. Gillard's FB88 units performed faultlessly in this role but weight was still found to be an issue with the 32-ton limit of the day. Later F12s, one of which is parked behind, were ordered in 4x2 configuration and utilised a 'bonus loader' for beam work. This clever device was effectively a swan-necked tag axle that provided a temporary 6x2 format and finally solved the weight issue for Gillard's. Rugby fans may be interested to know that these loads, pictured in June 1980, were part of the new Twickenham grandstand.

(Photo: Ray Gillard)

The car park of the Swindon county ground was a favourite change-over point for the numerous F88s of John G Russell. The units would trunk down from Scotland overnight and then await local drivers who would tip the loads throughout the south during the day. Given the intensive nature of this operation it was common for day cabs to be specified. The two sleepers in this line-up would have been in the minority. The day cab, along with the G88, was an option that first appeared on the F88 in 1970. Although a basic livery, the John G Russell fleet was very clearly marked with a large door transfer and a distinctive name board bolted onto the front of the trucks. Note that these three units are carrying brand-new containers.

(Photo: Adrian Cypher)

Many of Gillard's abnormal loads started out from here at the Bryco concrete works on the A358 near Henlade. Pictured here as they prepare to leave the yard, are three FB88 units including GMG 580N, now complete with Michelin Man and an F12. Route planning for one, let alone four of these massive eighty-foot loads, had to be meticulous, not only to minimise hold-ups but also to avoid causing any. Crossing four lanes of dual carriageway required considerable care from both the driver and bogie steersman, not to mention patience from other road users. Considering that two complete units have made the crossing already, the remarkable lack of tyre scrub marks on the road is a testament to the Gillard's bogie solution. A maximum speed of twelve miles an hour was usual for these loads and, once onto a motorway, the steering mechanism of the bogie would be locked up. Seen from this angle is a good view of the flat section air intake as fitted to the later TD100-powered F88. *(Photos: Ray Gillard)*

Being ex-Gillard's, GMG 580N was perfect for a second career as an underlift wrecker working with high-imposed loads at a slow and steady pace. On its previous beam work the load was carried on the fifth wheel, but as a wrecker the fulcrum was much farther back. To counter this the chassis was extended at the front to incorporate a generous tray which was liberally loaded with ballast, and the bumper was mounted ahead of that. When this picture was taken in the mid 1990s, the truck had just pulled a loaded Mercedes-Benz bulker from a ditch. *(Photo: Clive Davis)*

PMR 762M was new to Swindon transport in 1974 and is pictured soon after being commissioned. The simple red, white and black livery was very effective and highly recognisable on the road and, despite the nature of the work, the units were always well turned out. Later, a change in company policy saw the units sold to the drivers. The livery was retained but the headboards carried the name of the relevant owner-driver. *(Photo: Adrian Cypher)*

Curtis Mechanical Services bought this unit ready converted from a firm in Reading. The previous owner had built the lifting gear and bodywork himself using a 1975 FB88 240 as the base vehicle. CMS enjoyed good service from GEW 78N and only sold it in the early 1990s when a keen enthusiast offered them a deal they could not refuse. Interesting to note are the heavily ballasted bumper, which was filled with concrete, and the air vent modification beside the grille. *(Photo: Len Jefferies)*

The success of Chelmsford Heavy Haul can be attributed to two factors: the hard work of Philip Dyke and his dedicated team and the sterling service of the F88 tractors with which the company started in the 1970s. The all-Volvo fleet comprised up to twelve F88s plus a single F89. Philip was so impressed with the service of his System 8 trucks that Volvo has remained the manufacturer of choice ever since. This was the last example operated by Philip and was finally sold in 1987. Philip imported the FB88 in 1983 from Holland, where it had been part of a yellow-liveried milk tanker fleet, as the configuration was ideal for heavy haulage work in the UK. The unit was equipped with the TD100 engine, the 8-speed SR60 gearbox and a low-geared back axle that provided a low maximum speed of just 56 mph, but plenty of low-down lugging ability. Before the unit was put to work, it was re-plated to a hefty 70 tons by York Trailers and registered in the UK with the number plate UVW 253R that represented its correct year of manufacture. (Photo: Philip Dyke)

Jim Horn purchased UVW 253R from Chelmsford Heavy Haul in 1987. Jim, an owner-driver based in Scotland, bought the unit sight-unseen over the telephone. With just a coat of paint to tidy the cab and a lift axle pump from an old F86 to resurrect the rear axle, the 11-year-old unit was ready for its new role working alongside Jim's F7. At the time Jim's loads, mostly destined for Spain, included paper, paints, tyres, chemicals and specialised oil field equipment. Many of these loads were carried, roped and sheeted on flatbed trailers much to the amazement of continental drivers. In the first year alone the unit covered over 130,000 miles travelling the length and breadth of every main route in Spain. Problems were thankfully few. However, on one trip a failed differential bearing was shot out through the axle casing in spectacular fashion. The truck and trailer were left parked in a filling station while Jim returned with his other driver. On the next trip out, Jim and his uncle fitted a second-hand axle with just basic tools and a trolley jack, and it was snowing! The unit is pictured on one of its rare local jobs hauling telegraph poles in Grangemouth. Note the remnants of the original yellow livery still visible behind the grille. (Photo: Jim Horn)

Listen carefully and you can hear the fridge motors running in this atmospheric shot of Smithfield Market in the early hours. Many would consider the Scania 111 to have been the F88's most competent adversary. A further development of the already superb 110, the 111 proved to be a very, very capable and popular truck. Between them, the two machines carved out a massive slice of the heavy truck market in the UK for their Swedish manufacturers. The original 110 arrived four years behind the F88's predecessor, the L4951 Titan TIPTOP, and was produced, as the 111, for a further four years after the last F88. Although perfectly good machines, the Seddon and the ERF in this picture do seem somewhat overshadowed by the two big and glamorous Swedish cabs. Smithfield Market was a favourite haunt for Truck magazine's photographers in the early days as the magazine's office was just around the corner. *(Photo: Truck magazine)*

Not strictly a showman's truck but, nevertheless, this nicely presented F88 240 is pictured hauling what was an annual fairground load for GH Moreton. The South Wales based haulier would deliver this ride, belonging to Pat Collins, to Nottingham for the Goose Fair before moving it on to Hull the following week. This F88 was one of thirteen operated by GH Moreton in their smart, distinctive orange-and-white livery. The fleet's usual work was UK general haulage. Note the fitment of a chassis catwalk tank on this example. *(Photo: Malcolm Slater)*

In the 1970s the burgeoning fish stocks of the North Atlantic made fishing a hotly contested industry in those waters. Whatever the hostilities were at sea and between nations over the issue, once landed the fate of the catch was the same no matter who caught it: fast refrigerated transport to the markets or processing plants – almost the perfect role for this smart, Swedish-registered, 4x2 rigid. Note the extra spotlights and filled-in step holes in the bumper. *(Photo: AB Volvo Historical Archive)*

The green-liveried fleet of Joseph Fish & Sons worked from this yard next to Avonmouth docks and derived much of its work from that source and other ports in the Bristol area. This four-year-old F88 240, which worked alongside machines such as the Scammell Crusader parked behind, was in good shape when photographed in 1978. Despite the power and pace of the F88 240, operators could reasonably expect a unit employed on general haulage duties to return around 7 mpg with a 20-ton load, which wasn't at all bad for the time. Note the beautifully applied sign writing. *(Photo: Adrian Cypher)*

One unit that definitely comes under the heading of 'specialist vehicle' is this most interesting FB88 240 prime mover operated by the Titanic shipbuilders, Harland and Wolff. Although appearing very long, possibly because of the 40 cm shorter day cab and fitted bodywork, the chassis is actually that of a standard FB88. The squared-off front wings were, presumably, an in-house modification or repair. Note the heavily ballasted front bumper required to keep the front axle on the ground and prevent hopping under load. *(Photo: Len Jefferies)*

This superb F88 240 of Greenaways was employed on fridge work, with this stoutly constructed van trailer, between the company's base in Bude and the markets in London, hence the GLC exemption sticker on the bumper which allowed all-hour access to the city. TCV 22N, later sold to Aldridge Transport, is pictured southbound on the M5 in 1987 at the grand old age of twelve. Note the useful, but unusual, single side-loading door of the trailer. *(Photo: Marcus Lester)*

Stevens Amusements were big fans of the F88 and would eagerly purchase older examples for their purposes. This 1974 example raises mouth-watering possibilities as to its origin since it is that rarest of beasts, a UK-registered G88. Not only does it feature the set-forward front axle but also a day cab and quite possibly some of the original box van bodywork. All of this suggests a vehicle that may have started out as a wagon and drag combination employed on very high-cube loads. *(Photo: Malcolm Slater)*

H Frost and Sons are better known these days for a smart fleet of red-and-white units from Scania, DAF and MAN but there was a time when the trucks were painted blue and grey and were almost exclusively all Volvo. Frost's ran three F88s, two 290s and this very tidy 240 as well as numerous F86s. They were one of many operators that augmented their premium tractors with the less glamorous, though utterly dependable, F86, the nearest thing to a gaffer's motor that Volvo produced. Pictured coupled to a Ferrymaster three-axle, step-frame tilt, GLO 803N looks more than ready to assume the role of TIR express. The livery change came in the mid1980s, when a contract with Continental Cargo saw Frost's blue-and-grey units coupled in an unhappy marriage of colour with red-and-white tilt trailers. *(Photo: Colin Frost)*

ODE 644M was new to Mansel Davies & Son in 1974 and was purchased specifically to move aluminised steel from Pontarddulais to the north-west. The F88 240 had a remarkably long service and was finally laid off in 1990, having finished its career hauling tipper loads of stone for the Cardington by-pass. The unit is pictured in 1980 along with a Mansel Davies F7 near the transport café in Drefach. The company ran a number of F7s but the F88s were mostly replaced with F10s. *(Photo: Marcus Lester)*

John Billows, of Volvo dealership fame, originally ordered this stunning F88 240 to conduct a tour of Europe. The aim of the tour was to show what Great Britain had to offer the road haulage industry on the Continent. The F88 pulled a trailer loaded with aluminium truck accessories that included a complete tipper body by a young Mr Wilcox! A left-hand drive unit was deemed preferable for the trip as was the larger 90-gallon fuel tank to improve range. The Billows' paint shop applied the beautiful black livery and set it off by retrofitting an original chrome grille that had been languishing in the stores. Following the short three-week tour, the unit was offered for sale and found a new home with Brackmills who wisely decided to retain the stunning black livery. (Photo: Brackmills Haulage)

Brand new in 1974, NMW 396M was Syms' third F88 240 and joined the two earlier chrome grilled examples at the head of the fleet. This extremely tidy unit looks superb in the company's simple, but effective, two-tone livery and is pictured awaiting departure from the company's Calne depot with a neatly sheeted load. Note the spare ropes and sheet carried on the diesel tank and the rubber-edged rear wings.

(Photo: Adrian Cypher)

A traffic officer, part of the escort, inspects the insides of Flying Fortress, Mary Alice. The WW2 bomber made its final cross-channel journey with some major assistance. Harlow-based UKON trucking used three trucks in the move. The aircraft's fuselage was split in two and carried behind a couple of F88s, while a DAF 2800 handled the wings. Mary Alice had remained in France after the war and, along with other B17s, was converted for use by the French government to conduct extensive ground surveys and mapping of the entire country. Mary Alice is now part of the Imperial War Museum collection and is on display in the American Museum at Duxford. (Photo: Pieter Kroon)

N-registrations marked the end of the standard F88 240 for the UK market, as the new 290 variant effectively replaced it in 1975. In anticipation of this, Volvo uprated the F86 in 1974 with the TD70D engine which gave 201 bhp and 487 lb-ft of torque. While no match for the outgoing F88 240, the little F86 did provide adequate performance to those not wanting the massive power of the F88 290 at 32 tons. This close-up of Gillard's F88, XLL 874N, shows clearly the bolster arrangement on the fifth wheel, to which the load was directly mounted and chained. Also visible is the spare wheel that was carried in the centre of the chassis. Ever mindful of costly delays, this arrangement was the same on all of the FB88 units operated by Gilllard's while on this type of work. (Photo: Ray Gillard)

The G88 variant was developed in 1969 specifically for use in countries which operated the 'Bridge Formula' for weight, whereby the greater the distance between axles (the bridged length), the higher the maximum weight that could be carried. The new design came on line in 1970, with the G88 version appearing a little ahead of the G89. The heavy truck, trailer and multiple axle combination employed here seems a little over the top for this particular load. Note the British-manufactured Coles crane being used for the unloading of this cabin cruiser.

(Photos: AB Volvo Historical Archive)

Volvo F88s and DAF 2800s made up the bulk of UKON's fleet in the 1970s. The company's work was very diverse with continental groupage, plant movement and refrigerated loads being typical. The F88s, with TD100 240 engines, proved so versatile and reliable that UKON did not feel the need for the higher-powered 290 variant. However, more powerful Volvos did join the fleet in 1978 when the company started to buy F10s, equipped with a further refined version of the 290 engine: the TD100B. *(Photo: Pieter Kroon)*

A fine FB88 with lift axle performing a similar task to the F88s of Gillard's, but instead of the self-supporting load and bogie arrangement favoured by the English firm this Swedish operator is utilising a more conventional, though very sturdy, flatbed of extending trombone design. Of course, with the higher weights allowed on Swedish roads, this truck, unlike Gillard's FB88s, could also have worked happily on general haulage. *(Photo: AB Volvo Historical Archive)*

Not only did the compact day-cab option shave 400 mm from the bumper to back of cab dimension of the F88, it also reduced the overall height of the cab when tilted by nearly 300 mm, too. This was a useful consideration to any operator with restricted height in its workshops. This smart example operated by Svelast has a rather unusual trailer in tow. Essentially a flatbed, it features upright stanchions and a tailored top cover. Note the side repeater indicator behind the door. (Photo: AB Volvo Historical Archive)

Although this may seem a somewhat humble role for what was a premium truck at the time, this FB88 operated in Sweden would probably have hauled a drawbar trailer, too. The 6x2 bogie gave a 52/48 loading split between its front and rear axle during normal running, but the balance arm design utilised the reaction force of acceleration to transfer weight to the driven axle, giving extra grip when it was needed most. The same effect could be artificially induced by an activating arm attached to the balance bar, and that was the method used to raise the rear axle for empty running. (Photo: AB Volvo Historical Archive)

Despite its tilting ability, the F88 cab was only equipped with hydraulic tipping as an option. The original design was intended to be 'put over' by hand and was fitted with pre-loaded torsion bars at the front to ease the process. If the truck was fitted with the longer sleeper cab then stronger torsion bars were fitted to counter the extra weight. In either case it was recommended that the cab doors be opened to facilitate the operation. Once fully tilted, the cab would lock in that position on an arm which was fitted with a safety catch that could not be inadvertently knocked off. (Photo: AB Volvo Historical Archive)

This immaculate F88 and fridge trailer combination makes a spectacular sight in the simple two-tone livery of the Swedish ice cream manufacturer, Hemglass. Most of the company's distribution was carried out by an extensive fleet of delivery vans, from which, very often, goods were sold directly to the customer. This high-spec F88 would have been involved in the bulk movement of goods between factory and depots. The truck's air-conditioning unit and the generous diesel tank under the trailer for the fridge motor suggests that international loads into much hotter climes were also undertaken. Note the safety window and mirror in the passenger door and the wash–wipe system fitted to the headlights.

(Photo: AB Volvo Historical Archive)

From its humble beginnings in 1865, Cargill has grown into a major multi-national company in the foodstuff industry. Although a man of vision, it is hard to imagine that Will Cargill could have envisaged such international growth from his one original grain store in Iowa, USA. This well-presented F88 was part of the Dutch arm of the company and operated with this tri-axle, high-cube bulk tank. Note the non-standard diesel tank of the unit and the unusual mounting position of the trailer's lifting ram. *(Photo: AB Volvo Historical Archive)*

An FB86, with a GVW of 22.5 tons, could also have handled this tanker role, especially as nights out, which although possible in the smaller truck were best avoided, do not seem to have been on the agenda given that this FB88 is only fitted with a day cab. The front springs of the F86 were not progressive, unlike the F88's that slid on the rear brackets, which limited the front axle loading to 6.5 tons for the smaller truck. However, both designs were backed up by the same 2-inch shock absorbers. *(Photo: AB Volvo Historical Archive)*

The cross-over point between the F86 and F88 was a blurred one for some operators, particularly those in the UK with the 32-ton limit of the day. Although reaching the upper limit of its design at that weight, the plucky F86 was still capable of performing the job, and with its lower tare weight offered more payload. However, if journey times were critical – this was the time of change for driver's hours – then the bigger F88 was undoubtedly the best choice. This fine F88 employed on produce work makes a handsome truck with its lightweight aluminium van body and Trilex wheels.

(Photo: AB Volvo Historical Archive)

Between them, these two European-spec F88s portrayed one truck in the 2005 film, *The Da Vinci Code*. In a dramatic and terrifyingly realistic accident, the F88 obliterates a Citroen saloon, robbing the film's heroine of her parents and sibling. The truck with the framework over the chassis performed the main stunt and sustained the most damage. The framework was installed to mount a short section of bodywork which overhung the rear wheels to represent a trailer and give the impression that the truck was articulated. The second truck was for long-shot continuity with an actual trailer attached, though only the trailer's rear wheels made the final edit, and was damaged to match, although not so severely. The frame truck was a post 1975 model with the later brown interior, but both trucks were stripped of passenger seat and bunks. The cabs were reinforced up the A-pillars and the steering columns were braced against collapse with a sturdy strut to the seat base. Judicious use of 'frame advance' during the sequence reveals the Volvo lettering exploding from the service panel in the impact. *(Photos: Author)*

Take to the streets of Mayfair on a Saturday night with six premium tractor units and you can expect to attract a lot of attention and cause a fair amount of commotion as Truck magazine discovered in 1977. Having arranged for a special screening of the truck flicks White Line Fever and Duel the magazine provided tractor units to convey the various VIPs to the West End venue. This superb F88 240 belonging to Inconotrans joined a Fiat 170, Scania LB111, B-Series ERF, Ford Transcontinental and a Middle East veteran Leyland Marathon for the job. This 1973 unit, featuring an immaculate green-and-yellow livery, was another of the mid-changeover units with the new wiper location but old-style chrome grille. The night was not without incident and the F88 was in the thick of things. Here the air stack has just punched a hole in the glass canopy of the 'Curzon' cinema and later the unit was involved in an altercation with a Rolls Royce in Park Lane. Interestingly the 'Wardell' B-series tractor behind was the Union flag-bedecked ERF show truck of that year. (Photo: Truck magazine)

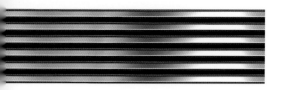

Volvo F89
More Muscle

Towards the end of the 1960s a power race was developing among the major manufacturers of heavy trucks in Europe. Fuelled by new legislation, such as Germany's 8 bhp per ton ruling, engine output for premium tractors was, for the first time, soaring over the 300 bhp mark.

Many of Volvo's competitors were now producing engines in this class, including big hitters such as MAN, Mercedes-Benz and Fiat. But, perhaps most worrying for Volvo, was home-grown competition Scania, whose mighty 140 model could deliver up to 350 bhp from its big V8 engine. However, Volvo had an ace up their corporate sleeve.

Designed only slightly later than the F88's TD100 engine of 1965, the TD120 was, by 1970, ready to make its debut. Another in-line six design, this turbocharged 12-litre unit could produce a healthy 330 bhp. At a time when many manufacturers still favoured large-capacity, normally aspirated engines of V8, V10 and V12 configuration, Volvo decided to stick to the formula that had worked so well in the TD100 of the F88. After all, a turbocharged straight-six engine was the lighter, more fuel efficient option and dynamically it was smoother running, better balanced and free of vibration too. Also, with great foresight of future legislation, it was much cleaner in its emissions and notably quieter in operation.

The home for this new engine was to be the F89. Billed as the 'Power Package', the F89 was justifiably thought of as a big-engined F88 but it was much more than that. It also featured a strengthened chassis, larger brakes, a stronger prop shaft and increased capacity in its oil and water systems to enable it to handle the increased power and far higher gross train weights of up to 100 tonnes. In the F89, Volvo had produced an extremely capable machine easily the match of those offered by the competition.

Outwardly, the new model was little different from the F88 except for a

new, full-width, black plastic grille that extended over the cab vents and 'F89' badges that were applied to the doors. There was also a new badge for the grille that stated '89-Turbo 6'. The F89 was the first vehicle to which Volvo applied this label. Interestingly, the 'Turbo 6' legend was later applied to both the F88's replacement, the F10, and the F89's replacement, the F12.

In 1969, in preparation for its application in the F89, the R60 gearbox had been beefed up and re-designated R61. At the same time, Volvo had introduced the SR61 which utilised a splitter to provide overdrive for all eight gears, thus creating the legendary 16-speed unit. For a year this new gearbox had done much to help the F88 keep up with its new high-power rivals and was well proven. Both gearboxes were made available to F89 customers, although it was the SR61 which eventually became standard fitment. In anticipation of the new model's heavy-haulage potential, Volvo also introduced the MR61 gearbox option. This combined the basic R61 gearbox with a torque convertor that increased tractive effort two-fold for each gear.

As with the F88, final drive was offered as either a double-reduction axle or, for heavier applications, hub reduction; the latter was available with the strengthened NR2 unit. Unlike the six-wheeled F88 chassis, there was to be no 'B' suffix applied to the F89; a chassis was merely referred to as 4x2, 6x2 or 6x4 depending on configuration.

But it was the TD120 engine that made the F89 what it was. As previously mentioned, the new unit had originally been designed just after the TD100 and actually used many of the same components. This was a calculated move by Volvo engineers that not only contained unit and parts costs for the bigger engine, but also made the F89 easy to repair and service by the extensive network of facilities which had sprung up throughout Europe in support of the F88. The main difference, besides displacement, was the adoption of an eight-bolt cylinder head design over the TD100's four-bolt system. This was necessary to contain the TD120's higher compression ratio of 15.0:1. The engine's maximum 330 bhp was achieved at 2,200 rpm and the hefty 933 lb-ft of torque occurred at 1,300 rpm. As with the TD100, a viscous thermo-coupling fan was employed to handle cooling of the larger radiator which provided the usual combined benefits of a fast warm-up with reductions in fuel usage and noise levels. In order to feed the turbocharger with the volumes of air that it required, a snorkel-type air intake arrangement was developed. This drew fresh, clean air from the airflow over the cab roof and channelled it down to a filter housing beside the engine. The air intake itself was of a neat and almost flat section design, which ran up the rear of the cab on the side opposite to the driving position. The same air-intake arrangement was applied to the F88 range at the same time.

Fitting the taller TD120 under the F88 cab was not easy. The only way to accommodate it without expensive alterations and re-tooling to the cab floor was to lean it over to one side. As this would encroach on such fundamental controls as the gear lever, it was decided that the inclination would have to be to the right. This was a natural choice for the designers, as Sweden had joined the rest of Europe in driving on the right and the left-hand driving position would remain unaffected. However, it did present one major drawback in that it ruled out a right-hand drive F89 for Volvo's largest single export market, Great Britain.

Inside, the cab was much as before with the same layout and controls as the F88 but with a new blue seat fabric and a blue quilted engine cover made of plastic. This scheme was also applied to the F88, which had previously featured a red seat fabric simultaneously. With the F89 expected to take on the mantle of long-distance super truck, there was a double-bunk option and also a TIR cab pack that provided the crew with such luxuries as a radio, wardrobe, carpets and a laminated table on the engine cover.

Detail changes to the F89 throughout its lifetime were few and usually in parallel with those that were applied to the F88. For example, both machines gained a useful three-way ventilation roof hatch in 1971 and two new grab handles at the base of the windscreen in 1973-4.

In addition to the F89 and G89 derivatives, Volvo also produced small numbers of an F89-based machine for the prestigious and somewhat challenging Swiss market. Designated CH230 (CH for Switzerland, 230 for 230 cm) this special narrow version of the F89 had its front wings taken back flush with the doors and utilised an F86 front axle to remain within Switzerland's strict 2.3 m width limit. As the Swiss operating weight limit was restricted to just 28 tonnes, the old, unmodified NR1 hub reduction unit was used at the rear. This version of the CH230 was produced only between 1977 and 1979. It was replaced by a new model in 1980, also designated CH230, which was a hybrid of modern F12 and F7 parts. All three variants gave a combined F89 production of over 21,000 units – a highly impressive figure for a premium tractor.

The F89 was a particularly rugged truck which was more than happy operating in extreme conditions. The reliability of the 330 bhp TD120 was enhanced by having most of the engine's auxiliary equipment gear-driven, including the vital water pump. Items that still relied on belts were carefully designed with inherent strength and longevity in mind. The 1300 w alternator, for example, featured enclosed slip rings to prevent the ingress of dust and dirt when operating in environments such as this.

(Photo: AB Volvo Historical Archive)

The angle of this photograph allows a good view of the F89's I-section front-axle beam. Manufactured by Volvo at the Umeå plant, this was a one-piece item drop-forged from a steel alloy. The front wheels rotated around a stout tapered kingpin supported at the top by roller bearings and at the bottom by a bronze bush. The wheel bearing itself was retained by a large nut at the outer end of the stub axle to prevent it sliding off in the event of a seizure or other failure. (Photo: AB Volvo Historical Archive)

This operator chose a day-cab G89 as the prime mover for a drawbar combination to maximise weight and load combinations on this cut-timber work. This interesting comparison of G88 and G89 models highlights how the full-width, black plastic grille radically modernised what was essentially the same cab. However, this situation was addressed in the 1973-4 updates which saw the F and G88 similarly equipped with a black plastic grille too. *(Photo: AB Volvo Historical Archive)*

This beautifully presented and high-spec F89 may seem all wrong in a role that, on the face of it, seems more suited to the F86. Indeed, Volvo produced a special high-torque, low-speed version of the smaller truck for this application. However, the operating conditions, being hilly and no doubt slippery in the wet, may have influenced the decision to put an F89 with 330 bhp and 6x4 drive on this type of work. Crews of contemporary machines in the UK may have looked on in green-eyed envy, but the ramifications of leaping in and out of an F89 cab with the frequency required of a refuse crew must be considered. *(Photo: AB Volvo Historical Archive)*

Although restricted to Sweden's heavy road system, which covered over three-quarters of the country by the mid1970s, the top weight/length category allowed for monstrous 6-axle 24-metre outfits, such as this hauled by a G89 variant, to operate at a whopping 51.4 tons. Because the F89 was engineered to cope with these weights but was sold to other markets with the same spec, it proved incredibly reliable and possessed great longevity at the lower weights of other countries. *(Photo: AB Volvo Historical Archive)*

The new grille for the F89, being full-width and made from black plastic rather than chrome, immediately set the model apart from the well-established F88. However, to emphasise the difference Volvo added a neat model-designation badge bearing the legend '89 Turbo 6' which was mounted below a re-worked version of the familiar Volvo logo that was now smaller and enclosed in a square border. Volvo opted to copy the wide grille look for the F88 290 when it introduced that model to the UK market in 1975 and fitted a revised designation badge reading, '88 290 hp'. *(Photo: AB Volvo Historical Archive)*

Running a 330-bhp tractor on general haulage back in 1975 with the 32-ton limit could have been considered a little over the top. However, although GER 403N was indeed on that type of work, it was just a stop-gap before it could be dispatched for its maiden voyage to the Middle East. Funstons had bought the 1975 F89 new that year specifically to take advantage of the growing trade on the so-called 'Gold Run'. It was the mountains of paperwork and red tape that conspired to keep the 4x2 unit on domestic work for three months. *(Photo: Funstons Transport)*

'Lorry of Arabia' perhaps. Pictured in the vast road-less location of the H4 in Jordan, GER 403N pauses for the camera while sporting some interesting local grille emblems. Note the all-important cab fan, which provided some relief in the absence of air conditioning. The Funstons unit also enjoyed minor celebrity status after appearing as the face of Kenprest retread tyres in 1978, the truck enjoying nearly half of the full-page advert.

(Photo: Funstons Transport)

This great shot pictures a well-travelled GER 403N parked up with an F88 290 of Welsh International Transport. The F88 290, being a UK market special, was perhaps a curious choice for Middle East work but was nonetheless a popular one. The original F88 240 had earned itself an enviable reputation in this theatre and the F89 was to build on that success. With its brick outhouse constitution and extra power, it really made the run its own. *(Photo: Funstons Transport)*

As GER 403N was proving its worth and with Middle East traffic booming, two more F89s were added to the Funstons fleet. New in 1977, the consecutively numbered MVA 369R and MVA 370R were both 6x2s with airlift rear axles. Funstons took this step to cut the risk of axle overloading and to assist traction in the difficult conditions which were frequently encountered. The new units were finished in a purple-and-yellow livery, later also applied to GER 403N, which became the colours for a generation of Funstons Volvos. Proud men, Noel Walker and Dave Ketteridge, pose with their new charge.

(Photo: Funstons Transport)

Two inevitable parts of the Middle East experience were snow and queues. It would often take days, even weeks on occasions, to clear a border. Drivers needed to be just as skilled at diplomacy as they were at driving when dealing with the officials whom they encountered. Bribes, known as 'Baksheesh', were commonly paid out to oil the wheels of negotiations and good firms sent their drivers with enough money to cover these inevitable costs. Both of Funstons' 6x2 units were equipped with the larger 90-gallon diesel tank. Note the snow chains hanging from the trailer. (Photo: Funstons Transport)

Pictured in 1978, MVA 369R and MVA 370R find some welcome shade during a trip together. By this time both of the six-wheelers, and GER 403N, had gained much needed air-conditioning units. Note Funstons' roll-top train/truck trailer, pulled by MVA 370R, designed to give tunnel and bridge clearance when loaded on a railway wagon. Funstons, like many others, would often load its trucks on the train from Munich to Zagreb, which saved on transit passes, diesel, wear and tear and also afforded the driver a useful break on the 9,000-mile journey. (Photo: Funstons Transport)

After the better part of ten years' service, Funstons disposed of their veteran 6x2 F89s. By that time the pair were somewhat tired and, in truth, were only fit for scrap. However, Peter Whitford saved them from that ignominious fate. Peter rebuilt both units and put them to work, replacing his F88 290. He later sold MVA 369R but retained MVA 370R. The unit was much altered over the years and could easily be mistaken for an F88 290 as it wore the deeper grille of that model. In fact the entire cab was taken from an F88 and, through some ingenious alterations to the gear linkage and cab floor, Peter created a right-hand drive F89. Changes to the chassis included new battery boxes, the relocation of air tanks and the replacement of the old multi-leaf springs for more forgiving parabolic items. Peter regularly ran MVA 370R to Austria for three years and the unit spent its final days with him on low-loader work handling impressive loads such as this, proving that there was still plenty of life in the old girl. *(Photos: Pieter Kroon & Author)*

MS White ran both F88s and F89s out of Canterbury under the 'White Trux' name. Loads were very much international and the Middle East was a favourite destination. Pictured descending into the docks at Dover is OJG 65R, a six-year-old F89 sporting the company's smart red, white and blue livery. The driver of this example has augmented the grille with the later-style VOLVO lettering of the F10/12 range. Note the very un-aerodynamic box on the roof rack. *(Photo: Adrian Cypher)*

Plain and simple, this very purposeful looking F89 makes a fine sight with its sturdy road/rail tilt trailer, even at rest, and the imagination can run riot with thoughts of the possible destinations reached by such an outfit. Photographed in the early 1980s, the 1977 truck was in great condition. Note the changed airtank arrangement, catwalk diesel tank, vacant spotlight positions in the bumper and missing bottom step on the driver's side, which must have made cab entry a little awkward.

(Photo: Adrian Cypher)

The standard of photography within the pages of Truck magazine was always extremely high, as is illustrated by this dramatic action shot of an F89 at close quarters as it storms across a stretch of Middle East desert. The great enthusiasm of the writers and photographers was particularly apparent in the publication's early years and was undoubtedly responsible for the huge readership that the magazine enjoyed. This picture was published in the November 1975 issue and accompanied an article on the pitfalls of running to the Middle East. The orange-liveried F89 was one of around thirty operated by Oryx Freight and the magazine rode with its driver, Pat Hawkes, for the 'Long-Distance Diary' in April 1975. It also featured in the September 1980 issue parked in the desert with an F88 240. The attendant story was about the decline of the British truck exports to the Third World markets that it had once dominated.

(Photo: Truck magazine)

Given that the F89 had developed a fine reputation as a Middle East tool, it is surprising to learn of Birdale International's unfavourable experience with the type. Birdale's mixed fleet consisted of artics and drawbars from Mercedes-Benz, Scania and Ford. The F89s were purchased new and suffered numerous problems, which, to its credit, Volvo always put right under warranty, but Birdale did not purchase any more examples. On one occasion the company's 108-tonne 6x4 F89 was towed six hundred miles to Doha for repair by a fully freighted Birdale Transcontinental. Note the desert-style ramp system used to load this example onto a semi-stripped tilt. *(Photo: Eric Wilson)*

This F89 6x4 unit was part of the mighty Sunters fleet based in Northallerton. Sunters, like so many others in heavy haulage, found that the F89 provided a very tough and capable off-the-peg solution to many of their requirements. This fine 1975 example, fitted with hub reduction, was operated virtually as supplied by Volvo with only the addition of a reinforced towing pin on the front bumper for push-pull, tandem running and manoeuvring of trailers. The livery was the usual Sunters mid-blue with yellow signwriting. *(Photo: Malcolm Slater)*

OA Brothers, based at London's Smithfield market, specialised in the International delivery of fine meat. Warm Mediterranean destinations, and beyond, were common, hence the air-conditioning unit fitted to the roof. The truck was also fitted with a catwalk diesel tank to supplement the 90-gallon item already fitted. Photographed in the mid 1980s, the 1977 unit was running at 38 tonnes and looked to be in good condition.

(Photo: Marcus Lester)

Polskie Linie Oceaniczne, the Polish state-owned shipping concern, made a tidy investment with these F89s in 1974-5. However, the company's pockets were deep and its negotiating power very strong as its

176 ships were moving around 5 million tons of freight a year during the 1970s. The PLO was established in 1951 and grew through the requirement for the movement of goods in an expanding post-war world.

The company remained under state control until 1999. Despite the rather austere, Eastern Bloc livery, the eight trucks look truly impressive.

(Photo: AB Volvo Historical Archive)

In this fine 'full frontal' view of an F89 it is possible to see, from the angle of the sump, the inclination that was required to fit the tall TD120 engine under the F88 cab. This was the reason why the F89 was only ever available from the factory in left-hand drive format. HOF 369 is pictured taking part in Truck magazine's Eurotest of 1975. This annual event was the ultimate test for premium tractors and in 1975 the F89 was pitted against Scania's 140, Saviem's SM340, ERF's NGC420, Mercedes-Benz's 1932 and DAF's frugal, but not so fast, FT2800 DKS. The F89, already a five-year-old design with an eleven-year-old cab, acquitted itself very well, finishing third in both fuel consumption and average speed, returning 52.42 litres/100 km and 59.46 kph respectively. The test truck was loaded with extras such as air conditioning and a headlight wash–wipe system, both of which became standard equipment on the F12 when it replaced the F89. (Photo: Truck magazine)

This work-weary machine started out as an F89 6x4 tractor unit in 1977, but was converted into a wrecker by WH Orchard of Cornwall to assist their scrap-metal business. Orchards opted to graft on the lifting gear taken from an ex-army Leyland Martian, an example of which is parked behind. However, not satisfied with that major surgery, they also decided to convert the unit to right-hand drive. The original F89 cab was converted too but the unit is pictured with a later replacement taken from an F88. When the author visited the yard in 1997, RWT 581R was awaiting a major refurbishment that was to include another fresh cab from an F88. (Photo: Author)

Another fine view of the 'HOF', Volvo's Truck Eurotest veteran, this time under going diesel trials in Sweden in conjunction with Fina Fuels. Truck magazine went to great lengths to maintain as near identical test conditions for all participants of its Eurotest programme. This extended to the same driver (Truck Editor, Pat Kennet) and the same route, fuel and tyres from the very first test in June 1975. The trailer was another constant with French manufacturer 'Trailor' providing an identical three-axle TIR tilt year on year. However, coupling problems did occur and the F89, with a 3.2-metre wheelbase, was the first truck tested with a different trailer; this Van Hool design of similar spec as provided by Volvo. (Photo: AB Volvo Historical Archive)

This smart G89 drawbar combination appears to be loaded with PRV V6 car engines. The PRV (Peugeot, Renault, Volvo) was co-developed to satisfy the requirements for the top saloon cars of each manufacturer; the 604Ti, 30TX and 264. The engine had an unusual 90-degree V-angle, a consequence of its original V8 format, and was never particularly good in its early years. Of the three manufacturers, Renault was alone in persevering with it and in the end developed a good engine for its Alpine sports cars, and even supplied a version for the ill-fated DeLorean DMC-12.

Note the additional rubber step pad atop the front wing that was fitted to G variants to facilitate cab access, which was made from behind the front wheel.

(Photo: AB Volvo Historical Archive)

A serious load of round timber for this 6x2 F89 operated by Ron Chaplin, as it heads south on the M5. The Volvo 6x2 set-up was often favoured over the 6x4 for forestry operations even in Scandinavia. The single axle was renowned for its good traction anyway, but with the 6x2 set-up, extra weight could be dumped onto it when the going got tough for extra grip. Note the unusual sun visor. *(Photo: Marcus Lester)*

Owner-driver LJ Joyce operated this smart metallic blue F89 from his base in Frampton Cotterall. PHU 313R, with 330 bhp and 16-speed gearbox, would have walked all over this single ISO container and its maximum 32-ton load. Although it has been removed, the grille would originally have carried the '89 Turbo 6' badge. The 'Turbo 6' legend referred to the fact that the six-cylinder engine used forced induction in the form of a turbocharger. This was later applied to both the F10 and F12. *(Photo: Marcus Lester)*

Barry Ives was no stranger to System 8 trucks as he was already running three F88 240s when he purchased this F89 from a scrap-yard in the early 1980s. The ex-Sunters tractor had suffered a broken crank and the engine was supplied in pieces. A comprehensive rebuild followed which included the fitting of the in-house designed and manufactured lifting gear. The huge boom was fabricated from H-section foundry steel with steel plates welded over for additional strength. The truck was also equipped with a Hiab unit, under-lift facility and winch, making it a truly versatile recovery vehicle. Often to be seen on the roads of East Anglia, this time to recover a hapless FL10, this fine machine could cruise all day at 50 mph with a fully laden artic in tow. The only drawback for this ability was a massive 4 mpg thirst, loaded or not, which was countered to some degree by the large non-standard diesel tank. Note the big 'A' logo carried on the rear locker, as Barry was an official service agent for Seddon Atkinson at the time. *(Photo: Barry Ives)*

NHY 209R started its career with John Golding but was bought second-hand by Heanor Haulage. Heanor were very keen on the F88 and F89 and ran around twenty-five examples at their peak. As previously mentioned, the only mechanical modification that the company felt necessary was the fitting of Fuller constant-mesh gearboxes. In the late 1970s Heanor built its own ultra-heavy units, the HHTs, which utilised suitably modified F88/9 cabs. *(Photo: Adrian Cypher)*

This impressive F89, operated by Stackhouse International Transport, was a Middle East veteran that was still hard at work at the time of this picture in 1990. As early as 1975, Ailsa Trucks, effectively Volvo GB, estimated that Volvos made up for 50-60 per cent of UK departures for the Middle East, which meant around 200 F88/9s at the time. Note that VFD 697S is fitted with an oversized diesel tank, possibly of Scania heritage. (Photo: Marcus Lester)

Another of Heanor's F89s, this time a 6x2 example, pictured in the company yard in 1982. Three-axle trucks in the System 8 range featured a strengthening sub-frame in the chassis rails above the bogie. On the F88/9 this insert was 9.5 mm thick, while on the F86 its thickness was 6.4 mm. The 6x4 chassis also featured a sub-frame of the same gauge above the bogie. This unit features a reinforced chassis, but like the hub-reduction axle it does not appear to be of Volvo manufacture. In common with most of Heanor's units, NBE 116R features the company-pattern bumper incorporating a sturdy towing eye and twin auxiliary driving lights. Note the subtle bracing of the sun visor. (Photo: Adrian Cypher)

In the 1970s Formula 1 transportation began to move away from its humble beginnings of converted bus or rigid lorry chassis and started to evolve into the highly developed unit and trailer combinations of today. System 8 Volvos were much in evidence in the early stages of this transformation with both Arrows and Brabham, the latter piloted by a young Tony Jardine,

using F88 tractor units. For Lotus, the most successful team at that time, it was somehow appropriate to go one better and utilise the services of an F89 instead. A late 1978 unit, XNG 60S reputedly arrived at Team Lotus through a Volvo connection with the Swedish racing driver, Gunnar Nilsson, who had previously raced for Lotus. The unit was an ex-

demonstrator and came with many extras such as air conditioning, heated mirrors, headlight wipers, auxiliary driving lights, 90-gallon tank and catwalk; it had also covered a mere 9,000 miles. An interesting feature is the factory-fitted spare wheel carrier that has displaced two of the four air tanks to new locations within the chassis rails. (Photo: Focalpoint)

Resplendent in the colours of 'Essex Petroleum', XNG 60S poses on the Lotus test track. This stunning livery followed the legendary black-and-gold 'JPS' years and aptly marked the company's arrival into the decade of excess that was the 1980s. The same livery was also applied to the first, limited edition, batch of Lotus's supercar, the Turbo Esprit. The purpose-built Crane Fruehauf trailer had the capacity to carry four complete cars loaded over work benches which ran the full length of the trailer. External underbelly lockers carried spare wheels, gearboxes and engines. A full load would run to little more than 7 tons, just like running empty for the F89. *(Photo: Focalpoint)*

Although Leggett's domestic work was carried out mainly with British trucks from manufacturers such as ERF and Seddon Atkinson, the European arm of the company made good use of F89s. This immaculate 1974 example was less than a week old when photographed in Cricklade high street and had yet to make its maiden voyage. Leggett European frequently ran to hot Mediterranean destinations including southern Spain and Italy and routinely fitted air-conditioning units – though not the slightly bulkier item offered by Volvo – for the comfort of its drivers.

(Photo: Adrian Cypher)

With modern standards of truck lighting it is easy to forget that in the era of the F89 this aspect of a truck's performance was something of a lottery. Although good, the F89's headlights were compromised by having the high/low and sidelight functions all in a single unit when other manufacturers were starting to split them into two-lamp systems. Spotlights mounted in the bumper were a common addition to many F88/9s but Volvo also offered the distinctive spotlights seen here mounted above the bumper. To allow the lights to remain flush and protected by the bumper, a special version of the drop-down service panel, with recesses for the lamp's bowl, also needed to be fitted. *(Photo: AB Volvo Historical Archive)*

This impressive extending low loader with five axles and rear steering capability seems very appropriate behind this rather splendid 6x4 F89. When developing the F89, Volvo's engineers could call upon the services of a special 'dynamic' test trailer. With the outward appearance of a baulker, the complex machine actually housed a 500-bhp hydraulic retarder that drove the 6x4 bogie on which the trailer ran. Electronic controls fitted to the test truck could be used while in motion to simulate load, through resistance, in varying degrees. In heavy-haulage applications, ballasted F89s working as prime movers were recorded moving loads of up to 250 tons. Note the replacement diesel tank. (Photo: David Wakefield)

Edwin Shirley Trucking, already big fans of the F88, purchased two F89 tractors new in 1976. RJO 767P and TJO 712P impressed very much with their big torque and rugged reliability. The left-hand drive format was not a problem either as EST units would spend many weeks at a time on the Continent with a single tour. Indeed, despite the availability of right-hand drive on the later F12, many EST examples were ordered as left hookers for just that reason. The EST livery, illustrated here in the slightly less imposing Mark 1 version, did much to establish the company. Customers and concert-goers soon came to recognise the striking units at venues throughout Europe. Here the two units come head-to-head at a sports stadium in Cologne in 1976.
(Photo: EST)

To complement their numerous F88 and F89 tractors, Radclive Transport also ran a number of F89 drawbar outfits. This superb 6x2 example was the company flagship in the early '70s. Radclive, like many Middle East experts, found that drawbar combinations could offer improved flexibility and, with careful planning, could save money too as on split loads the trailer, once empty, could be parked and left until collected on the way home. Note that the trailer is connected to the truck via a fifth-wheel dolly arrangement.

(Photo: Adrian Cypher)

Three F89s, shiny and new, ready to deliver thousands of miles and years of service to a new owner. The road haulage industry worked differently when the F89 was introduced: trucks still tended to be purchased outright rather than leased and operators would routinely expect to run trucks beyond 5-10 years of age. Trucks of this era were designed to meet these expectations, with varying degrees of success. Volvo's products proved to be particularly good in this respect, something that reflected in the strong residual value of second-hand examples.

(Photo: AB Volvo Historical Archive)

This wonderful photograph shows a purposeful CMR 593L poised at the company's Faringdon base as it awaits departure for a trip to Italy in 1974. Both the F88 and F89 possessed a generous steering lock, as is illustrated here. The system was servo-assisted and load-sensitive, giving more assistance in relation to resistance; however, driver input would increase to maintain feel for the given situation/circumstance. Note that this 4x2 F89 chassis was fitted with a neat twin 66-gallon tank installation that provided a useful range of 800-900 miles. *(Photo: Adrian Cypher)*

Crouch's orange recovery fleet is a familiar sight to many and the diversity of equipment operated is impressive. This tough-looking F89 was fondly remembered as one of the best vehicles the company had ever owned. The 1976 6x4 unit originally started life as a tractor for Plant Haul of Bedford who often used it for continental work, hence the TIR plate still worn on the bumper. Crouch's added the Holmes 750-recovery crane and bodywork when they purchased the unit and put it to work, otherwise unmodified. During a long and illustrious career it proved itself more than up to the job and, on one occasion, performed a recovery from Switzerland. Note the weight cradle that has been attached to the front bumper to compensate for heavy loading on the rear.

(Photo: Len Jefferies)

Mick Moody took the plunge as an owner-driver in 1973. His first truck was a 1971 F88 240 which worked solely on UK general haulage for several years but in 1975, with work at home becoming harder to find, Mick took the plunge and accepted a load destined for Saudi. This winter load was a baptism of fire but truck and driver came through in one piece. By the middle of 1976 Mick had become a regular on the Middle East run and, by choosing his loads and customers carefully, was making a success of the 'Gold Run'. By now the F88 was becoming decidedly second-hand with each of the punishing 9,000-mile round trips taking a further toll on the five-year-old unit. Having been pleased with the Volvo, Mick decided to 'up the ante' and purchased a brand-new 4x2 F89 in the knowledge that the extra power and left-hand drive would be positive advantages. The new blue-and-white unit did not fail to impress and, after a short running-in period on UK work, was soon delivering diverse loads of 'Western goodies' to distant destinations throughout the Middle East. Note the plastic drums for drinking water that were carried on the roof rack, the Arabic script on the bumper and catwalk diesel tank. *(Photo: Truck magazine)*

FJO 522S, a late-example F89 registered in 1978, was a Middle East veteran originally owned by Radclive transport. Pictured in 1982 the unit was by then owned by John L Kent and operated out of Bristol. F89 tractors could be specified with a wheelbase of 3.2, 3.4 or 3.8 metres. The longer wheelbase of this has allowed room for the inclusion of a chassis locker aft of the diesel tank. Note that the operator has added a panel of fine mesh to the middle of the grille on this example. *(Photo: Marcus Lester)*

Volvo trucks accounted for a large proportion of the Hallett Silbermann fleet line-up of the 1970s. This highly impressive F89 not only featured double-drive with hub reduction but also the optional cyclone air cleaner and stack for improved engine breathing. Volvo offered this high-capacity unit at the time, mainly for operation in dusty environments such as the Middle East. When specified, it replaced the F89's standard item with a cylindrical version that remained outside the cab and joined a large filter housing on the chassis before being trunked through to the turbocharger. Many of Hallett Silbermann's F88s and F89s were fitted with an additional cat-walk type diesel tank as seen here, although in this case it is mounted further back than usual to clear the large air cleaner housing. Another interesting feature of this vehicle is the individual rear wings. *(Photo: John Maybury/Hallett Silbermann)*

The Transport Development Group (TDG) was good to its name in the 1970s and evolved a strong heavy-haulage division from one of its numerous acquisitions, Econofreight. The ranks of the Teesside operation were swelled in 1980 with the rescue of the Anglo-Dutch company, Magnaload. The deal included all of Magnaload's hardware including two F89s, RAJ 530R being one, and a Scammell Explorer. The three trucks were painted in the familiar blue-and-white livery while the whole fleet was re-branded as Mammoet-Econofreight, Mammoet being the Dutch part of Magnaload. RAJ 530R often operated as a ballasted prime mover but is pictured here as a unit in the mid 1990s when still active as a shunter. *(Photo: Clive Davis)*

With its rugged mechanical components and strong performance, even the oldest F89 could be usefully worked as shown by this Dutch-registered example that was at least 35 years old when spotted working near Rotterdam in 2008. Originally a drawbar and perhaps still operating with a trailer, the truck was in remarkable shape, requiring little more than a tickle with a paintbrush to appear considerably younger. Note that the driver preferred to view the offside mirror through the windscreen, pushing the mirror arm fully forward to achieve this. The truck also has an additional, and robust, tow-pin, probably for the manoeuvring of a drawbar trailer. *(Photo: Clive Davis)*

With the breadth of England to cross before even reaching the Continent, top-of-the-range tractors have always been popular with Irish operators on international work and, attracted by the performance, the F89 was no exception. This fine example operated by Brendon Myers is typical. Note that this unit carries another 90-gallon tank mounted on the offside, the batteries and air tanks being relocated to new positions within the chassis.

(Photo: Marcus Lester)

Looking very purposeful with a TIR tilt in tow as it heads down the M4, this handsome and well-travelled F89 running at 38 tonnes was operated by JD Fairweather. As well as F89s the company also ran a good number of F88s, including an early chrome-grille 240 example, on its continental work which often included tilts for Norfolk Line.

(Photo: Marcus Lester)

This particularly robust looking F89 had a 17.7-ton load capacity as a solo rigid from its chassis with the proportions of an articulated unit. The 6x4 chassis was also available with a 4.2- and 2.6-metre wheelbase, providing load platforms of 6.9 and 7.9 metres respectively. In each case, as the length grew, the load capacity was reduced by 100 kg. Note that due to the proximity of the load platform to the rear of the cab, this unit is not fitted with the normal snorkel air stack.

(Photo: AB Volvo Historical Archive)

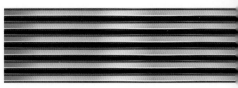

Volvo F88 290
The GB Special

By 1975 the F89 had been available for five years. Although UK operators were using examples successfully, these were mainly on long continental or heavy-haulage work where the driving position was less important. The left-hand drive only format still ruled it out for a large number of potential buyers who did not venture beyond UK shores, but whose work could use the extra performance that the F89 offered over the F88 240. Many had no alternative other than turning to those manufacturers that could offer F89 performance in a right-hand drive package. Volvo knew that the situation would eventually be resolved with the F89's replacement, the F12, which would be available with right-hand drive, but the launch of the F10/12 range was still some two years away. If Volvo were not to lose customers and credibility it would need to address the problem much sooner.

The only avenue left open was to provide the F88 with substantially more power, just for UK customers, until the right-hand drive F12 became available. The answer came in the shape of the TD100B, an engine developed in Sweden by the team of turbocharging guru Bertil Haggh. Bertil was an early advocate of the turbocharging principle and had been largely responsible for steering Volvo's engine policies down that road in the early 1950s with the original TD96. Based on the 9.6-litre TD100, the new engine used the latest turbocharging knowledge to produce well over 300 bhp before the big thermo-coupling fan cut in but, even then, 290 bhp was readily available. This was obviously stretching the capabilities of the original TD100 so, in an attempt to maintain reliability and extend component life, the engine's characteristics were radically altered to produce a slow, controlled burn which gave the pistons a progressive and sustained push rather than a sudden blow. To achieve this, the engine used different pistons with a new three-ring design, the top ring being retained by substantial iron inserts, and a revised injection system that featured a

new pump with larger-diameter elements to deliver the fuel over an extended period. Although the bore and stroke were unaltered, the volume of the combustion chamber was increased and the compression ratio lowered to 12.5 to 1. The changes in injection and combustion were maximised by fitting the latest, state-of-the-art turbocharger, developed in the UK by Holset. This finely tuned combination created such a complete burn within the cylinders that the engine could achieve California's strict pollution criteria for 1976.

As the engine would be peaky and best at high rpm, a back pressure regulator was installed to improve low-down response. Volvo was already fitting such a device to great effect on the revised TD70D of the F86. Attached to the rear of the turbocharger, the regulator restricted the passage of exhaust gases to create synthetic engine load, which made the turbo work harder and push more air/fuel into the cylinders. The regulator also provided an exhaust braking effect which was activated whenever the brake pedal was applied. Of course, the design also included a separate exhaust brake activated by a floor switch.

Because the new engine ran faster (2,400 rpm) and therefore hotter than the original TD100, particular attention was applied to the cooling and lubrication systems which were increased in capacity by around 33 per cent. The larger, thermostatically controlled fan and an oil cooler of the F89 were fitted but less obvious were new cylinder liners with a corrugated outer profile to present a greater outside area and thus more contact with the water of the cooling system and important revisions to the cam and crankshafts. The larger fan was enclosed in a specially developed shroud which was deeper than the F89's so the old flush-style grille had to be replaced with a new design that gave more clearance. Although the radiator and fan assembly were no wider than before, Volvo designers wisely decided to extend the new grille out over the cab air vents. At a glance, this clever piece of marketing gave the F88 290 a similar look to the F89, immediately differentiating it from the standard F88. In fact it was the F89 grille that was used but, to give it the necessary clearance, it was mounted in an additional plastic shroud. Also changed, and for the same reason, was the service panel below the grille. On the F89 and the standard F88 this item was vertical and flush but for the F88 290 it now had to adopt a slight angle. The only other outward difference was a new, cylindrical air intake that was mounted, as before, on the rear of the cab opposite the driver. Topped with a mushroom-style rain guard, this high-capacity item was required to feed the big turbo and, at a casual glance, was not dissimilar to the 'Cyclone' system which could be specified on F88s and F89s for operation in dusty conditions.

The 16-speed SR61 gearbox was fitted as standard. As with the F88 240 and the F89, the range control was on the gear lever itself offering high and low versions of the four main gears with the splitter control mounted on the side of the centre console where it felt readily to hand in a natural sweep from the gear lever. The remote splitter control worked so well that it was retained for the original F10/12 in 1977 and was not amalgamated onto the gear lever until 1982.

Lastly, to maintain reliability with all the extra power and torque of the new engine, the 290 was fitted with the F89's propshaft, wheels and brakes.

The result of all these changes was a truly dynamic performer that changed the parameters for 32-ton operation in the UK. Although it did not possess the sheer grunt of the F89, it was not far behind and the F88 290 was ultimately faster at the top end. The combination of the high-revving engine and the 16-speed gearbox translated into devastating on-road ability that few could match.

The unfortunate downside to all this performance was a reliability record that just couldn't match the levels that the TD100 and TD120 enjoyed. Much of the criticism levelled at the new engine was due to the excessive smoking which occurred following a cold start, the blame for which usually fell on the back pressure regulator. The engine and turbo did carry various components to alleviate the symptoms and there was also a protracted starting sequence but the problem still persisted. Now, with the benefit of hindsight, many think that intercooling the TD100B would have cured these problems. Unfortunately that technique was still in its infancy in 1975, although Volvo were well advanced in its testing. To the company's credit, Volvo stood by the F88 290 and offered generous extended warranties to operators.

As the basic design of the F88 was twelve years old by the time the 290 was introduced there were to be no more changes over its brief two-year production life. However, soon after its launch the entire System 8 family all benefited from new, cosier interior trim with brown fabric for the seats and brown carpet replacing the blue quilted vinyl on the engine tunnel. At the same time the centre console which housed the radio and heater controls gained a black finish.

Overall the F88 290 was a superb and logical development of the F88 and made an ideal compromise to the F89 problem in the UK for Volvo.

What might have been! These two photographs show an early prototype of the UK-only 290 model complete with unusual styling changes to the front access panel, bumper and lighting arrangements. All these changes were driven by the need to accommodate the bigger fan and shroud assembly that was required to keep the new TD100B engine cool. While this prototype is interesting and historically important, the author cannot help but feel relieved that Volvo found a way to adapt the more familiar face of the F88/9 to accept the changes made behind. In a marked move from the standard F88 and the F89, the 290 adopted, even at this early stage, the cylindrical air stack that was to become a key-identifying feature of the model. In this installation it also features the final production version of the mushroom cap where some other prototypes were fitted with a much larger item. The Swedish registration BEM 742 also appeared on one of the evaluation prototypes, a truck of normal F88 290 appearance.

(Photos: AB Volvo Historical Archive)

London's Smithfield Market in the wee small hours and two fine examples of Volvo's new secret weapon in the power race – enter the F88 290. By 1974, Great Britain had become the biggest single export market for Volvo and the Swedish company knew that it must address the problem of being able to supply its top tractor, the F89, in left-hand drive format only. The new model was designated the F88 290 after the output of the new TD100B engine which actually produced over 300 bhp before the fan cut in. With the 16-speed SR61 gearbox and all that power, the 290 soon gained an enviable reputation for its performance. The movement of perishable goods was one obvious role and the new model soon became a popular choice for those hauling refrigerated loads over long distances. (Photo: Truck magazine)

With long distances and extremely tight schedules between venues, speed and the power to maintain were vital characteristics for EST trucks then as now. The F88 290 fitted the bill perfectly. Apart from being one of the first examples registered in 1975, GWL 44N was also the first truck purchased outright by EST rather than leased. This angle gives the best view of the new model's grille, the main feature distinguishing the 290 from all other F88 and F89 types. Parked next to GWL 44N in this impressive line-up of EST Volvos is WJO 699R, perhaps the finest example of an F88 operated by the company. *(Photo: EST)*

This time the venue is London's Royal Albert Hall and the unit is the 1977 F88 290, XJO 913R. Just visible behind the roof rack is the top of the cylindrical air stack with which this model was fitted. Together with the grille and service panel, the air stack was the only visual difference from the F88 240 and F89. A capacity load for the EST F88s was usually only around 12 tons but tended to be extremely bulky and required high-cube trailers to accommodate it. Step frames were normal with ramps favoured over tail lifts for speed of loading. Trailers always ran on air suspension to protect the delicate loads and were limited in height to 3.5 metres to fit under continental bridges. *(Photo: Truck magazine)*

This fine colour shot of WJO 699R shows just how beautifully the dramatic Mark 2 EST livery was applied to this particular unit. This is perhaps why it featured in so much of the company publicity and literature at the time, particularly the renowned company calendars. The unit also enjoyed a full-page picture, complete with a leggy model, in the large-format book, Trucks and Trucking, *published by Octopus in 1979. Many F88 drivers took styling ideas from WJO 699R, such as the chrome V on the grille, to personalise their own trucks.*
(Photo: EST)

This fine FB88 290 was new to Hallett Silbermann in 1976. The unit featured a 6x4 chassis with hub reduction and was based at the company's depot in Hatfield. Pictured fresh from the paint shop and with the headboard still empty, this commissioning shot with impressive load illustrates well the type of work this vehicle would have undertaken. Note the fitment of a catwalk diesel tank and neat one-piece rear wings.

(Photo: John Maybury/Hallett Silbermann)

Having operated a long list of domestic and Anglo-American machinery, this tidy F88 290 marked something of a departure for Swan's Transport of Strethall, Essex. The big Swede, with its power and sumptuous cab, was something of a revelation too and another was purchased soon after. Swan's have remained with Volvo trucks since, having progressed through F10s to FH12s. Pictured taking part in the 1981 Saffron Walden Carnival, NCE 120R is seen providing traction for the float of LPA Industries which, by strange coincidence, was a Viking longboat that year and also numbered 8 in the procession! *(Photo: S Swan)*

Late in its career at Swan's, NCE 120R suffered an unfortunate accident that saw the unit flipped onto its side while tipping a load of grain. The cab was subsequently replaced and therefore in remarkable condition when it arrived at the Duffield's Dealership for trade-in against a new F10. This did not go unnoticed by Duffield's Rod Hammond who set the unit aside for some special PR work before it was to be sold on. This simple but effective green-and-yellow livery will be recognised by fans of the 'Canaries' as the colours of Norwich City Football club and it was as the 'Canary Flier' that the unit performed promotional work at the Norwich ground. Next stop for NCE 120R was Kings Lynn Speedway where, with the same livery, the unit was used to promote the activities of the track bearing the legend 'Sunshine Stars' in its headboard. Following this glamorous interlude, NCE 120R was sold to an owner-driver who put it to work on contract to Norfolk Line. *(Photo: Rod Hammond)*

In the 1970s and '80s the yellow-and-black F88s of Brackmills were a common sight with loads of impressive shapes and sizes. Here, SVV 866R an FB88 290 with double-drive and hub reduction, is seen tackling the movement of a narrow-gauge railway engine. Although the weight of this particular load would not have caused a problem, the choice of this particular prime mover plus a three-axle trailer suggests that the job may have involved some difficult terrain. Despite being loaded it looks as if the driver of the London Brick Mammoth Major is champing at the bit to get past. *(Photo: Brackmills Haulage)*

Owner-driver LJ Joyce operated this smart F88 290 from his Bristol base on continental work before progressing to an F89. With its additional catwalk diesel tank and well-loaded roof rack of tarpaulins and water containers, LGB 238P (pictured in 1978) looks every inch a continent-crushing TIR express. Note the unusual ladder access to the roof rack which is over the rear corner, neither item being Volvo pattern. *(Photo: Adrian Cypher)*

This two-year-old F88 290, towing a low-capacity, single-axle, four-wheel trailer with a negligible part load of pallets, was possibly a demonstrator for the Volvo agent, Wincanton Garages, at the time of this picture in 1977. Note how the all-encompassing Wincanton livery extended to the grille's mesh and housing, somehow softening the presence of this usually striking item. *(Photo: Adrian Cypher)*

This very smart and early F88 290 was registered in 1975 and was a company flagship for Phelps and Davis. The company employed it on continental fridge work from its Wiltshire base. With Italy a common destination, the unit bore the fleet name 'Roman Emperor' and is pictured at the company's yard in Westbury in 1978. Note the wide spacing of the bogie on the period trailer in this shot. (Photo: Adrian Cypher)

In 1975, when the F88 290 was launched, Volvo's European service points numbered a whopping 536. In Britain alone, Volvo held 7 million pounds worth of stock which equated to £700 for each of the 10,000 trucks it had registered in the UK. No other manufacturer was making such a large commitment to its customers and products. This allowed Volvo to claim almost 97 per cent availability of spare parts at any given time. The entire operation was managed by a computer system that was able to spot trends and even anticipate seasonal demand. At the close of 1974, Volvo were able to claim that at no time that year were there more than ten trucks off the road for more than ten hours. It was superb back-up of this nature that allowed drivers and operators of trucks like this magnificent drawbar combination to sleep easily at night. *(Photo: David Wakefield)*

Edwin Shirley Trucking's striking Mark 2 livery was first applied to the company's F12 tractors which started to arrive in 1978. The Elizabethan purple, canary yellow and EST blue combination was a brave and bold statement. The livery was so well received that it was retro-applied to the rest of the fleet, GWL 44N being an early convert. The livery was another aspect of a company with its finger on the pulse. From humble beginnings, in the harsh economic environment of the early 1970s, the company quickly prospered by servicing the exacting requirements of the rock music industry on tour. Bands such as Genesis and the Rolling Stones were early customers and the fleet quickly expanded from the original rented F86 and trailer to meet demand. GWL 44N is pictured at rest on Wansted Flats, showing off the livery which gave the EST units pin-up status for a generation of young enthusiasts such as the author. *(Photo: EST)*

When the curtain finally came down on its last performance for EST, GWL 44N passed into the very capable hands of Rushden-based haulier Arthur Spriggs. For the majority of its working life with this company, GWL 44N tipped tilts throughout the UK for Thrapston Warehousing but is seen here unusually coupled to a box van. Interestingly the under-bumper bar, used for mounting the number plate and driving lights was removed when the Mark 2 livery was applied by EST. Just visible is the top of the centrally mounted exhaust stack that the unit gained in later life. The title 'ED PINK' referred to Edwin Shirley and their livery and was bestowed on the unit by its new owners as a fitting tribute to an illustrious past of rock and roll. *(Photo: Frank Chessum)*

'Simply stunning' is the only way to describe the superb livery that was applied to GWL 44N for its retirement. Now the company's dedicated show truck, this was actually the second special paint scheme that was applied. The finish and detailing, inside and out, are astounding and it is plain to see why the unit has done so well at truck shows over the years. Note the Viking warrior mascot mounted on the headboard, a fitting and apt addition. *(Photo: Frank Chessum)*

Arthur Spriggs' normal livery at the time, seen here on another F88 290, was a common sight throughout the UK and Europe applied to various Volvos and Scanias and is little changed to this day. RVV 280R, a 1977 unit, was fitted with the larger 90-gallon tank that provided over 150 miles extra range, very useful on long continental journeys. Apart from offering increased range, the bigger tank looked more purposeful and better filled the chassis. However, it did unfortunately develop a reputation in later life for rust problems with the internal baffles. The unit is pictured coupled to a tilt trailer of Thrapston Warehousing back from or destined for, the Continent. (Photo: Frank Chessum)

In the author's hugely biased opinion, OYC 774P was the finest F88 that ever graced the Queen's highway. It was trips as a boy in this very vehicle with his then brother-in-law, Terry Bright, that started his passion for the F88. Ray Keedwell started his haulage business in 1969 with one old Seddon tractor unit. By the time the author was introduced to the fleet in the late 1970s the numbers had reached around twenty units and was an exciting mix of tractors from Volvo, Scania, Leyland, Seddon Atkinson and even Berliet, a veritable feast for a young truck enthusiast! OYC 774P, an F88 290, was bought new in 1976 and given the fleet name 'Blue Mule'. It was Keedwell's third F88 although the other two were both 240s. The unit is pictured in the Leigh Delamere services on the M4 with an impressive load of timber. This was a handsome truck featuring Keedwell's fine livery with half-moon signwriting. Note the paint detailing to the wheels and the intricate pin striping applied to the bumper and wings. (Photo: Adrian Cypher)

Another fine view of 'Blue Mule'. In this later picture, dating from around 1980, the unit has undergone a complete re-paint (which included the Michelin Man) and has new horizontal signwriting. Sadly some of the finer detailing, such as the white wheel nuts, was lost at this point. It has also been fitted with a large diesel tank, taken from a Scania, to enable return trips to Harwich to be made without refuelling. The Baulker trailer was the only one on the fleet and was purchased specifically for a regular shuttle run for Fisons between Somerset and Ipswich. At the time a large amount of Keedwell's traffic involved the haulage of bagged peat compost taken from the Somerset Levels, which took the fleet all over the country. Back loads would be anything going but often included timber, sugar beet, hay and paper. The author's best memory of 'Blue Mule' was a three-day trip double running with Keedwell's TL12-powered Leyland Marathon. Happy days!

(Photo: Marcus Lester)

Late in 1975 Volvo unveiled what was to be the last major update of the venerable F88/9 and, although the range had just a couple of years left to run before replacement, it was to be the most significant update of the cab since its first appearance on the L4951 Titan TIPTOP in 1964. The most striking difference was the introduction of new brown fabrics for the seats, bunks and additional upholstery which, combined with the new carpeted engine tunnel and black-finished dash and console, gave the cab a warm and cosy feel. There was also more insulation and double-skinned seals for items such as the gear lever to further reduce interior noise levels from controls which passed through the floor. Also new was an optional lidded document tray, tailored to the shape of the engine tunnel, which provided a useful tabletop when closed. The new bunk fabric created a snug birth and the attractive block pattern and a very similar design was carried over to the F10/12. A new set of warning lights, mounted in raised housing above the main instruments, gave the impression of a flight deck rather than a truck, a feature that amazed the author as a child. Note the fabric cushion plug for the rear window aperture and the removable hanging wardrobe.

(Photos: AB Volvo Historical Archive)

Brackmills developed something of a reputation for the movement of railway engines in the 1970s and '80s. In this case it was the turn of VNV 374S, a late-registered F88 290, to move a relatively small 0-4-0 engine using a two-plus-two axle arrangement. Brackmills reported very good service from the TD100B engine. Indeed, with a thirty-strong Volvo fleet equipped as such, it confirmed the theory held by many that a hard-worked and well-serviced example could be every bit as reliable in service as the legendary TD100.

(Photo: Brackmills Haulage)

This well-worked FB88 6x2 of White Trux is pictured as it enters Dover with this unusual outbound load. This company specialised in Middle East work and it is thought that, once into de-regulated areas, they would often run Australian style road trains with three or more trailers behind their F88s and F89s. Note the generously proportioned catwalk diesel tank and the spotlight holes in the bumper that were cut by the operator, the holes being bigger than the factory would make. (Photo: Adrian Cypher)

Terry Stephens, founder of Bristol-based Western Tyres knew that he had stumbled on the perfect vehicle for his high-cube loads when he spotted this European-specification F88 drawbar outfit in Holland. Despite having stood idle, and somewhat neglected in a field for some considerable time, the TD100 engine was readily coaxed into life with a fresh set of batteries and a deal was quickly struck. Upon its return to the UK the outfit was sent up to the Volvo plant in Irvine for type approval and registration, gaining the 1979 'V' plate. Although fitted with a UK 290 grille, the European F88 specification of 'Blue Max' meant left-hand drive and a flat-section air stack. *(Photo: Terry Stephens)*

By 1981, BHT 69V had gained the usual blue-and-white livery of Western Tyres and the roof rack had been removed. 'Blue Max' gave Western Tyres four years of reliable service, delivering and collecting loads throughout the UK and Europe. When sold, it was snapped up by another tyre dealer that ran it for a number of years on similar work. In later life the tilt bodywork was removed and the truck operated as a solo rigid with a blue-and-yellow livery. Note the additional larger tank mounted in front of the standard 66-gallon item. *(Photo: Marcus Lester)*

This extremely smart F88 290 was one of a number operated by FC Tomlinson and is typical of this well-presented fleet then and now. VRY 268S, pictured in 1982 taking part in a Classic Commercial Motor Show at Cranfield, carries an unusual, demountable tanker on its flatbed trailer, one of two such combinations operated by the company. Tomlinson were also keen participants in the early days of European truck racing, campaigning OHS 420P, a somewhat older F88 290, during the 1985 season.

(Photo: Adrian Cypher)

NAD 634P was bought new by Febry's Transport in 1976 and was three years old when this photograph was taken at the company's base in Chipping Sodbury. Febry's also ran several second-hand F88 290s on this bulk powder haulage work using these impressive trailers equipped with self-unloading capability. Febry's livery, though just one colour, was nicely set off by the shadowed signwriting and delicate panel pin stripes. Note the rubber-edged metal rear wings. (Photo: Adrian Cypher)

An F88 by Royal Appointment? Pictured as it circles the Victoria Monument at the end of The Mall, London, in June 1976 is HNK 647N, an early example of the 290 model. As with many of the Hallett Silbermann fleet, this 4x2 unit was not just restricted to heavy haulage and low-loader work. Silbermann's also handled a large amount of general haulage that would often include tilt trailers to Europe and beyond – hence the TIR plate worn by this well-travelled unit. Being specified as a fast road tractor, to perform the latter role, too, this particular F88 was equipped with the SR61 gearbox and the double-reduction rear axle. *(Photo: John Maybury/Hallett Silbermann)*

This 4x2 F88 290 was another of Hallett Silbermann's more versatile units capable of general haulage or, as here with this tracked crane, moderate heavy haulage work. The double-reduction rear axle, manufactured in-house by Volvo, was a strong unit capable of both fast road cruising and handling train weights up to 50 tons. Note that the fifth wheel seems to be mounted on a substantial sub-frame, perhaps to gain the correct height for this type of swan necked trailer. (Photo: John Maybury/Hallett Silbermann)

Probably the most heavily modified and specialised FB88 in the country is Yeoman's awesome prime mover, 'Southern Comfort'. For many years this mighty machine wowed the crowds at truck shows while still being a bona-fide working truck. Until 1982, OWS 948R led a relatively normal existence for a 6x4 unit working on heavy-haulage applications. However, all was to change when its second owner put it up for sale. Paul Hammond, an F88 enthusiast, had been looking for a suitable heavy tractor to provide dedicated emergency cover for the movement of his company's shovel loaders. Breakdowns on these machines were not common but a failure would render his fleet of Volvo tippers expensively redundant until a replacement was provided. This insurance easily offset the price of having a second-hand truck kicking around the yard so Paul

was happy to part with £12,000 for the five-year-old unit. Developments started almost immediately with a cab stretch, executed by Brian Rolls, to provide the two-man crew with more living space, and the application of the special black-and-silver livery. While performing its intended role for Yeoman, the eye-catching unit started to attract much interest and soon Yeoman's telephone was ringing with heavy-haulage inquiries. Taking on outside work meant that OWS 948R would be away from base even more and so, once again, the unit came under the knife to improve crew accommodation. Inspired by the recent purchase of an F12 Globetrotter, it was the cab roof this time that attracted Paul's attention. The original was cut away and replaced with a massive high-rise item that was fabricated in-house from steel. The cavernous interior was lavishly

appointed with tailored wood cabinets and beds. The steel roof extension lasted for six long years, but was eventually replaced by a dimensionally identical version made from glass fibre. With the crew accommodation sorted, Paul turned his attention to the mechanics of the old FB88. More power was obviously desirable and the local Volvo dealer was convinced that fitting the latest F12 engine and gearbox was a viable idea. The result was a useful 400 bhp from the intercooled 12-litre engine, which was transferred via the new gearbox to the original 6x4 back end. Now plated at a massive 150 tonnes, the unladen weight with the French Nicholas trailer is 48 tonnes alone. 'Southern Comfort' is an awesome sight and still a crowd favourite wherever it goes – especially if hauling one of Paul's vintage Scammells. (Photo: Len Jefferies)

Despite the high-waisted doors, the F88 provided the driver with good all-round visibility. The large glass area behind also made for a light environment in which to work, especially in day-cab form, thanks to the close proximity to the driver's shoulder of the large rear window. However, many drivers, such as here, preferred the cosy feel and privacy afforded to them by keeping all the rear curtains drawn. This handsome F88 290 was five years old and operating at 38 tonnes with this tri-axle tilt when photographed descending Jubilee Way into Dover. Note the Scania 'Super' badge on the grille. *(Photo: David Wakefield)*

Michael Rolls started his haulage business in 1960 with an ex-RAF rigid Ford truck which he converted into a tractor unit. This was followed by a noisy Commer two-stroke and then later a Leyland Beaver. Over the years the business developed and started to specialise in heavy low-loader work. The blue-and-white fleet became a familiar sight throughout the country often with impressive and dramatic loads. Pictured in 1980 and slightly work-worn is one of the five F88 290 tractors that were operated by Rolls. The type was much favoured and gave no major problems over very long and arduous service lives. The enormous crated load in this picture was a jet engine baffle, used to suppress the noise of a running engine while being ground-tested, and was on its way to RAF Lakenheath. Note the fitting of an additional diesel tank on this unit. As there was no factory part offered for this location it was common practice to cut and shut a standard 66-gallon item for the purpose. The displaced batteries, along with the fourth air tank, were relocated within the chassis rails. *(Photo: Mick Rolls)*

An F88 290 with an interesting history is VEE 692V, which was owned and operated in Essex by Gerald Barton for over 25 years. Originally a 1977 unit, it was leased from the John Hebb Volvo Dealership and spent six months operating out of Immingham docks on Middle East work. However, payments to Hebb's stopped and the unit disappeared only to surface six months later parked in Cheddar marketplace with a cracked gearbox casing, bald tyres all round and no passenger seat. Eighteen months of legal wrangling followed after which the unit was repaired and re-registered, hence the 1979 V plate. It was subsequently offered for sale; Gerald was first in line and purchased the unit for £15,000. By the time this picture was taken in 1996, VEE 692V was much modified, running an FL10 short block and F10 rear axle. The original gearbox with a new casing was, however, unchanged apart from a new set of bearings. The cab was kept in order with regular strip-down and re-sprays undertaken by Gerald. As it was employed almost exclusively on tipping grain, the chassis was fitted with a hydraulic oil tank in the location of the batteries for the trailer's telescopic ram. Note the home-made mirror shields to fend off the overhanging branches of rural lanes, the non-original spotlights in the bumper and the reverse-reading VOLVO badge.

(Photo: Author)

The stringent maintenance schedules applied to the Rolls fleet extended to regular cab repainting which helped to keep the F88's weak spot in fine fettle. Here, despite the rigours of heavy haulage and advancing years, LNH 864P still looks superb in this photograph from 1987. The impressive load here is a pair of oil coolers for a transformer which, as they are being transported dry, actually weighed very little, perhaps two tonnes each at the most. *(Photo: Jack Nowland)*

For the toughest jobs, where axle overloads or traction could be a problem, Rolls could depend on RLL 618R, an FB88 290 with 6x4 drive. The low-down lugging abilities of the SR61 gearbox fitted to this unit were further enhanced by hub reduction on the rear axles.

This, the commissioning photograph for RLL 618R, was taken at the redundant Bourn airfield in 1977. At the end of its time with Rolls this unit was sold to fellow heavy-haulage experts and Volvo fanciers, Robinson's of Sandy in Bedfordshire. Robinson's mildly customised

the unit and then worked and showed it for a number of years before selling it on to GJ Vincent of Fraddon in Cornwall who repainted the cab in a stunning blue metallic livery. *(Photo: Jet Photographic)*

Ciba-Geigy was one of many own-account users that operated F88s. The performance and reliability of the Volvo had not gone unnoticed in this sector and fleet managers were keen to capitalise on it. There was also a benefit to be had in the high-profile status enjoyed by the F88. To be seen delivering your own product to a customer's premises with 'the' tractor unit of the day was, for many, too good an opportunity to be missed. When Ciba-Geigy first purchased Volvos, it brought to a close a forty-year history of operating British trucks. Drivers were transferred to the new machines straight from the fibreglass cabs and crash gearboxes of Scammell Handymans. How pleased were they with this upgrade! This fine close-up shows KVE 59P at rest, though presumably not in its local Cambridgeshire countryside. Though far from elaborate, the Ciba-Geigy livery of blue and yellow was very distinctive and units were always well presented. The tank trailers were used for bulk delivery of the company's famed liquid wood glue, Araldite. *(Photo: Ciba-Geigy)*

Pictured leaving the company's Duxford plant, KVE 59P was one of the first F88s purchased by Ciba-Geigy in 1976. The unit just visible in the background as it enters the site via the weighbridge is most likely KVE 58P as it was usual for units to be purchased in pairs. The Volvo trend continued for Ciba-Geigy with the F88s being replaced with F10s and those, in turn, with the later FL10. *(Photo: Ciba-Geigy)*

This very tidy F88 290 was one of a number to run in the smart red-and-black livery of AA Griggs. Although the company HQ was in Cambridgeshire, KVA 627P, along with other units, was based at a sub-depot in Watchet, Somerset. From here it was employed mostly on contract to the paper mill at St Regis. Waste paper loads were delivered in and finished paper reels taken out to destinations throughout Great Britain. Pictured in 1983, the seven-year-old unit looks in fine fettle with fresh paint and no apparent rust (so often the Achilles Heel of the F88 cab) and heads up a neatly roped and sheeted load of paper reels. (Photo: AA Griggs)

John Davies started out as an owner-driver back in 1976 with an old AEC Mammoth Minor twin-steer unit. This was soon replaced with his first Swedish truck, a Scania 110, and that soon after by a second-hand F88. Both impressed John and his small fleet grew steadily with both marques represented in equal numbers. It was only after the closure of his local Scania dealer that John standardised on Volvo. Bearing the appropriate bumper legend, 'She smiles at the miles', is GFC 340S. This stunning 1978 F88 290 shows just how well the simple and elegant blue-on-blue livery worked on the handsome and purposeful lines of the Volvo cab. This unit, pictured coupled to an immaculate European-spec tri-axle tilt fitted with super single wheels, was also fitted with the big 90-gallon main tank as well as the catwalk item. The Davies' F88 units, much like those of EST, were routinely fitted with a trademark arrangement of four auxiliary lights mounted under the bumper with a protection bar running underneath. (Photo: Davies International)

Towards the end of 1993 John Davies, in a nostalgic mood, decided that the time had come to add an old F88 to his fleet of modern F12 and FH12 tractors. A search of the local small ads resulted in the purchase of this fine late-model F88 290. The 1978 unit had been leading a charmed life for some time having apparently been used by an enthusiast as his personal transport. Mildly customised inside and out the unit was in superb condition, particularly the cab that on an ordinary working F88 would have been well into its second or third flush of youth. A mechanical overhaul and the fitment of a new fifth wheel (the original had been removed) saw the 15-year-old unit through its test. The next stop was to have been the paint shop for application of Davies' now blue-and-white livery. However, fate intervened when an F12 went sick and VTA 872S was pressed into service and dispatched to the Continent with one of the company's many smart Gray and Adams tri-axle refrigerated trailers. The trip was completed without a problem and on its return the unit was given the blue-and-white livery. (Photo: Davies International)

Pictured westbound on the M4 in 1989, and looking in tidy condition for an 11-year-old unit, is Starr Roadways' F88 290, PFD 567R. Based in Bilston, this unit was tasked with the movement of Starr's road-building plant. With the extra urge from the 290 engine the fine handling characteristics of the F88/89 became even more apparent, especially when compared to contemporaries such as Ford's Transcontinental with its soft-sprung cab. This sure-footedness allowed rapid progress to be maintained even on the twisty bits. *(Photo: Marcus Lester)*

R & G Transport originally owned LOD 493P, pictured here with a good load of pallets on this twin-axle, four-wheel trailer as it approaches the Severn Bridge, but by 1979 it was employed by Keep-Um Trucking, a subsidiary of Frank Robbins Transport. Note that a second 66-gallon tank, which looks rather good in this location, was fitted to this F88 290 on the offside.

(Photo: Marcus Lester)

An atmospheric early morning start for WWV 947S as it prepares to leave the Rolls depot in Bourn, Cambridgeshire with a 1938 Leyland Metz fire engine destined for classic vehicle dealer, John Brown. Rolls first purchased F88 tractor units because the engine power and weight combination available were very well suited to heavy and abnormal loads in an off-the-shelf package. This particular unit, fitted with the Volvo-built double-reduction rear axle, remained a key part of the all-Volvo fleet right into the new millennium and was kept up to snuff for shunting duties and emergencies until the business was sold to Hallett Silbermann in 2001. *(Photo: Mick Rolls)*

LOD 493P, this time pictured in the mid 1980s, and now converted to a 6x2 format with an after-market tag axle conversion. This gave the old 1976 unit the *flexibility to operate at 38 tonnes with a two-axle trailer, as here, or, at a lower tax rate, with a three-axle trailer. This allowed Keep-Um Trucking to run the truck* *for many more years following the UK's new weight limit that was adopted in 1983. (Photo: Marcus Lester)*

Bearing a very apt headboard title for an F88 290 is JTC 421P. This 1976 unit, operated by Coronline Transport, was photographed in 1981 at the Avon Truck rentals yard in Chipping Sodbury. The F88 cab, in common with most of its contemporaries, suffered from side-window fouling when conditions deteriorated. Air deflectors mounted beside the headlights were commonly fitted to alleviate the problem and also became something of a fashion statement too. (Photo: Marcus Lester)

Running trials of the F88 290 were vital to its development and a number of pre-production prototypes were placed with trusted hauliers, such as Siddle Cook, both in the UK and Europe. However, much of the initial proving was carried out at Volvo's state-of-the-art testing facility in Hallered. Hidden deep in a Swedish forest, the facility was opened in 1973 at a cost of 5 million pounds and was subject to stringent security that even extended to a designated no-fly zone overhead. Almost every conceivable road condition had been created, including a section of heated road to provide summer conditions in winter.

The last of the F88/9 models crossed over with the new F10/12, this FB88, for instance, was registered one digit later than PKT 928S, an early F12 operated by Edwin Shirley Trucking. (Photo: David Wakefield)

Laura Ashley was another own-account user that favoured the F88 for its performance, reliability and status. Two examples, both TD100B-powered 290s, were operated from the company depot in Powys and delivered to destinations throughout the UK. Driver David Rowlands spent eight happy years behind the wheel of VWD 127S. First registered in 1978, this 4x2 unit originally ran in this burgundy-and-black livery with its own dedicated York trailer. At that time Laura Ashley had no single livery with all vehicles operating in different colour schemes; the older F88 NVE 911P, for example, was finished in cream. *(Photo: David Rowlands)*

When the time came to present a standard corporate image, an inspired decision led to Paris Green getting the nod for the haulage fleet. When this deep, lush colour was combined with the silver chassis paint and subtler sign writing, the effect was both dramatic and very classy. Both the F88 290s received this new livery but unfortunately NVE 911P was written off in an accident soon after. Many years later, Dilwyn Williams of Gribbarth Quarry saved VWD 127S for preservation. *(Photo: David Rowlands)*

Even if the trailer doesn't do the unit full justice, TJ Sweeting's smart livery looks superb applied to this 1975 F88. GAF 67N was actually a TD100-powered 240 that started out with John Williams (English China Clays) Ltd of St Austell. The retro-fitting of the 290 grille to a 240-powered F88 was a common practice.

However, this subterfuge rarely extended to replacing the flat-section air stack with the correct cylindrical item, although some strange alterations have taken place in this case. (Photo: Marcus Lester)

With a low October sun setting on TWE 815S, Wyatt International's long and happy association with the F88 draws steadily to a close. Pictured in 1986 this was the last in a long line of F88 units operated by the Norfolk-based family firm and was finally sold a couple of years later to a preservationist in Redcar. The strong performance and reliability of the F88 forged a loyalty to Volvo products for Wyatt's and such was their belief in the F88 that this unit, a late-model 290, was unusually purchased second-hand and late in life to bolster the numbers of a far more modern Volvo fleet. Originally a 4x2, it was modified with a tag axle, large Scania diesel tank, an upright exhaust system and a wiper-mounted windscreen washer arrangement.

(Photo: Author)

The TD100B of the 290 variant carried various equipment aimed at making the engine user-friendly. One of these components, the exhaust pressure regulator, was originally developed for the TD70 of the F86. The regulator restricted exhaust gas flow to increase combustion temperatures at light loadings. This fine example illustrates well how a coat of matt black paint behind the grille could benefit the look of the unit. Light-coloured liveries in particular benefited from this simple attention to detail. Note the four-in-line trailer, a type that, due to its oscillating axles, gave great stability on uneven surfaces and cambers. It was also thought to improve mpg figures and tyre life.

(Photo: Marcus Lester)

This interesting day-cab F88 290 was actually used on continental work by The Fatstock Marketing Company (FMC) which absorbed The Harris Bacon Company but continued to operate it as a separate entity with the original name and livery. Presumably loads were mere channel hops with the lorry returning the same day.

OLB 180P is pictured taking part in a round of the Lorry Driver of the Year competition in 1979 held at Longleat. Note the early aerodynamic aid. (Photo: Adrian Cypher)

If the registration number seems familiar, it is because HHW 235N started out with Phelps and Davies in their smart blue-and-white livery (see page 93). Pictured in 1982 the unit was, by then, part of the equally smart red-and-white liveried fleet of C&B Haulage. Paddy Conroy and Brian Burgess liked their F88s, both 240s and 290s, and a good second-hand example was always welcome on the fleet. Note that the unit now has a catwalk diesel tank. *(Photo: Marcus Lester)*

This smart, late-model F88 290 had started out as part of the mighty fleet of F88 units that were operated by Dawson Freight, the haulage arm of Volvo dealers Dawson Commercial. The next owner for FJO 515S was Alan James, a Swindon-based owner-driver. Pictured early on in its new career with an impressive load of round timber, the 1978 unit is still wearing the blue chassis paint and hazard-striped bumper which was common to the majority of the Dawson Freight F88 units. *(Photo: Paul Perris)*

Paul Perris, a self-confessed F88 nut, went to work for Berkshire-based C&B Haulage straight from school. Paddy and Brian looked after the enthusiastic youngster and, when his age and experience allowed, put him behind the wheel of bigger and better trucks. On gaining his coveted Class 1 licence Paul achieved his goal and was handed the keys to his first F88. That was followed by SLN 65R, this magnificent 1977 290 example. Paul cherished this unit and personalised it with many accessories of the period including the continental style roof rack with ubiquitous Michelin Men, forward flaps and those EST-style grille flashes. *(Photo: Paul Perris)*

Paul had been aware of Alan James and FJO 515S for some time and through regular chats on the CB he found himself first in line to buy the unit when it came up for sale in 1993. Some of the risks associated with becoming an owner-operator were alleviated by an arrangement for Paul to work exclusively for his old employers, C&B Haulage, as a sub-contractor. As such, the unit received the familiar red, white and black livery. The resemblance to Paul's old unit, SLN 65R, by now sadly written off, is clear to see. Apart from Paul's considerate driving style there was no kid-glove treatment for FJO 515S with the unit taking on any job thrown at it. Further developments made by Paul were the fitting of a second upright exhaust stack, stainless steel straps for the 90-gallon tank and a custom-made tool locker which was mounted between the chassis rails at the rear of the unit. As FJO 515S was so well known from the show circuit, prospective buyers were many when it was time to sell in 1997 but it was to be Bedfordshire-based HE Payne who finally bought the unit for preservation. *(Photo: Paul Perris)*

Although the F88 290, like most of its contemporaries, was equipped with a separate exhaust brake, the exhaust pressure regulator, fitted to boost power at light loadings, would automatically be engaged with the service brakes to give a similar effect. This FB88 290 of John Foster features an interesting chassis variation with the air tanks having been positioned in the battery location, although the reason for this is unclear as no additional fuel tank has been fitted in behind. The 290 should have breezed this lightweight load in 1984. *(Photo: Marcus Lester)*

Scania's LB110/11 was always pegged against the F88 and usually with a few bhp more but having less gears the on-road performance was very close. With the introduction of the 290 in 1975, Volvo's product took a mighty leap ahead. Scania answered this in 1977 with the introduction of the DS11-02 which produced 305 bhp. This 1975 F88 290, a rare second-hand purchase for Syms, was something of a flagship among the company's other 240-powered F88s. The unit was originally supplied through Wincanton Garages – hence the triple-G suffix registration. *(Photo: Adrian Cypher)*

A once familiar livery that is now sadly missed is that of Kammac Trucking Ltd seen here beautifully applied to an impressive F88 290 as it ploughs down the M4 in 1982. Although pulling an exceptionally tall curtainside trailer, which would appear normal behind a modern FH-series Volvo, especially one with Globetrotter roof and full air-kit, this picture does emphasise just how far truck design, particularly in terms of height and profile, has advanced since the glory days of the F88 and its contemporaries. *(Photo: Marcus Lester)*

THE MIDDLE EAST CAB

VOLVO
Trucks available for demonstration

VOLVO F86 4x2 Tractive unit
VOLVO F86 6x2 Robson drive
VOLVO F86 8x4 Tipper
VOLVO N10 6x4
VOLVO F88 4x2 Tractive unit

For the top manufacturers of trucks in the 1970s the Middle East had become something of a benchmark. A vehicle's popularity and sales in all markets could be reflected by its successful adoption by operators on this harshest of runs. By the mid 1970s, with competition from manufacturers such as Ford with its big new Transcontinental, the System 8 cab was in need of improvement to keep it competitive until the new F10/12 range could take over. In line with other manufacturers, Volvo introduced a package of optional accessories designed to make the driver's life safer and more comfortable. In the case of Volvo this package was introduced as the 'Middle East Cab'. The range of features, actually developed by Ailsa Trucks, included a combined fridge, cooker and sink unit with a 25-gallon water supply that occupied the passenger compartment plus air conditioning, night heater, wardrobe, document locker, spotlights, air horns, heated

mirrors, anti-lock brakes, sun visor, stone guards for lights and windscreen, cab alarm system, gearbox range inhibitor, fire extinguishers, headlight wash–wipe system and much more. This motor show example of the package has been fitted to the right-hand drive F88 290 of a Scottish haulier. There were a number of drivers who preferred to stay on this side of the cab while travelling to and from the Middle East. Many felt happier in treacherous mountain ranges, such as the Tahir in Turkey, when they could see the edge beneath the wheels and keep an eye on the sheer drops. Furthermore, with horrendous head-on accidents being all too common, once out of Europe the right-hand drive cab also provided drivers with a few more feet of safety from on-coming local traffic which would often be very badly driven. (Photo: Truck magazine)

This McAlpine FB88 290 looks superb at the front of this King low loader with its Caterpillar grader load. Pictured in 1982, the 6x4 unit with hub-reduction axles rests with a McAlpine F10 or F12 at the Leigh Delamere services on the M4. Although the TD100B of the F88 290 was something of a 'special' brewed up for the UK market, it became virtually the standard engine for the F10 in all markets when that model replaced the F88 in 1977. *(Photo: Marcus Lester)*

The dividends of a smart livery and meticulous attention to detail are perfectly illustrated in this photograph of the last three F88s to work for Tom Shanks Trucking in the late 1980s. Flanking the wonderful TAM 489 are two beautifully turned out F88 290 variants resplendent in TST's intricate livery. The 1975 unit on the right, GNV 225N, worked for many more years following its sale to a trailer manufacturer. Night vision was never an issue for Tom Shanks' drivers with each unit equipped with eight spotlights in this trademark fashion. *(Photo: Tom Shanks)*

Davies Turner is a success story with a rich history dating back to 1870. Over the years this independent company has diverged into all areas of transport and shipping. Motorised transport was introduced in 1914 and the company was among the first to operate TIR services and to embrace containerisation in the 1960s. This FB88, operated out of the company's Battersea Wharf depot, plied routes to distant continental Europe and the Middle East. Note the wacky angle of the sun visor, perhaps a victim of the 290's legendary pace to which the bumper sticker refers: 'Speed on Bro, hell ain't half full'.

(Photo: David Wakefield)

The engine thermostats of the TD100B were set at 81 degrees C and until that temperature was reached the big fan assembly, taken from the F89, would remain still leaving the driver with around 312 bhp, a figure not far behind that of the F89 itself. This very smart F88 290 operated by EuroDrive was photographed in 1982. Despite its Continent-hopping routine it looked in fine condition for a well-worked five-year-old. Although red, rather than the more usual black, the sun visor on this unit was still the official item offered by Volvo at the time. *(Photo: Marcus Lester)*

'Mother said there would be days like this.' An early winter's morning in Pentons' yard and every driver's nightmare. However, even the harshest of British weather was well within the capabilities of the F88 which was designed to contend with the Scandinavian climate. Its winter traction was particularly good and F88 drivers would often find that they could negotiate conditions that others could not, even without the aid of snow chains. There was also that excellent cab heating system with the two separate units. By the time the yard cleared of smoke, your F88 290 would be as warm as toast. *(Photo: Stephen Penton)*

By gradually developing UDH 652R over the years, Pentons were able to keep the unit working profitably alongside their much newer machinery. One of the earliest upgrades was the addition of a third axle to allow flexibility at 38-tonne operation. Further major detail changes came following an extensive refurbishment of the entire unit that saw the addition of a larger diesel tank, a Scania air deflector, twin upright exhaust stacks and an air stack of the later F10/12 type. It was also decided to remove the cab's side windows. Note the interesting curtain-sided (Tautliner) refrigerated trailer used to facilitate the unloading of palletised chilled goods.

(Photo: Stephen Penton)

By 1982 this F88 290 was pulling baulkers for Charles Eady & Son Ltd of Marlborough, but could the air-conditioning unit and the 90-gallon tank point to a more exotic past of continental trips? Note the mirror shield fitted on the nearside to fend off the advances of overhanging branches encountered by the unit while collecting loads from farms off the beaten track on the Wiltshire plains. *(Photo: Marcus Lester)*

XRP 600S would have been a very late-model F88 that was actually registered after the first of the F10 replacements for the model. With operators and drivers keen to get their hands on the new Volvos when they became available in 1977, there were many cases of later-registered F88s, mostly 290s, available from dealer's stocks. Good deals were to be had and those cautious of new models did well to boost their fleet numbers with F88s. Note that this example has been fitted with an F10/12 tank in later life. *(Photo: Adrian Cypher)*

An exotic load for this F88 290 of exotically named 'Exonia European'. The specialised field of boat delivery is fraught with problems, especially when running to the Continent with its low bridges, etc. Being a reliable performer, the F88 was a safe bet in this field and meant one less worry for the operator. Note the large diesel tank fitted to this unit, presumably to limit the number of times the load had to be squeezed under garage canopies. *(Photo: Adrian Cypher)*

This tidy F88 290 of LEP Transport not only advertises Hatcher components in its headboard, it also displays a good number of their after-market additions, including the sun visor, spray deflectors, chrome wheel-nut covers, air horn and headboard itself. TNG 22R was less than a year old when photographed in 1978 and made an impressive TIR outfit with this matching twin-axle tilt. *(Photo: Adrian Cypher)*

Owner-driver Mike Taylor from Paddock Wood in Kent offered traction only with this mildly customised F88 290. Unfortunately the fitting of the 'West Coast' style bumper did away with the original lower step making it quite a stretch to the second. However, this addition did give the unit a distinct look. Note the Viking mascots mounted on the roof rack and top mounted spotlights. Was Mike ahead of his time with the latter addition? *(Photo: Marcus Lester)*

Dave Dickson's very smart F88 and tipper combination was kept busy on a mixed diet of agriculture, aggregate and scrap work but would also run tilts to the Continent on occasions – hence the TIR plate. Although wearing a 290 grille, GMO 554K was actually a 240 example registered some four years before the 290 model actually became available. Originally it would have worn the chrome grille. Note that the original 240 air stack was retained. Dave replaced the Volvo with an equally well turned out DAF 2800.

(Photo: Adrian Cypher)

The author finally realised a childhood dream in 2008, some thirty years after his first encounter with an F88, when he got to drive this beautifully preserved example that passed through the hands of vehicle restorer,

Ashley Pearce. ROG 47R was a particularly apt example as it was a late-model 290 with brown interior and single bunk, sparking memories for the author of sleeping across the seats and engine tunnel of RT

Keedwell's example. Handling was everything it had always been described as – taut and controlled and much like a giant go-cart. *(Photo: Author)*

You probably wouldn't be reading this book had it not been for RT Keedwell running the F88 that the author encountered back in the late 1970s. So it seems hugely appropriate to end with Clive Davis's wonderful homage, THU 332M. The unit was new to the Distillers Yeast Company of Bristol in 1973 and remained with the company into the 1990s, finishing its long career as a yard shunter. Clive acquired the truck in 1998 and set about the painstaking restoration himself which was topped off with the period Keedwell livery. *(Photo: Clive Davis)*

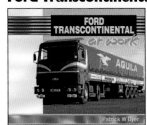